MASTERPIECES OF
ENGLISH FURNITURE
AND CLOCKS

AN EASY CHAIR
with walnut frame upholstered with original floral needlework covering of exceptional design.
Temp. Queen Anne
(Collection of J. S. Sykes, Esq.)

MASTERPIECES OF ENGLISH FURNITURE AND CLOCKS

A Study of Walnut and Mahogany Furniture, and of the associated crafts of the Looking-glass Maker and Japanner, together with an account of Thomas Tompion and other famous Clock-makers of the 17th and 18th Centuries

BY

R. W. SYMONDS

Illustrated by 8 plates in colours and 130 from special photographs of examples chosen from private collections

Introduction by

JEROME PHILLIPS

Published by

STUDIO EDITIONS
LONDON

Originally published in 1940 by
B.T. Batsford Ltd, London W.1.
in an edition limited to 1250 copies only
This edition is published in 1986 by
Studio Editions, a division of
Bestseller Publications Ltd.,
Princess House, 50 Eastcastle Street,
London W1N 7AP

Publisher's Note
The text of *Masterpieces of English Furniture and Clocks* has been
reprinted without alteration. The publishers would like to
make it clear that the ownership attributed to all the furniture
and clocks illustrated in the text was that at the time of first
publication in 1940.

ISBN 1 85170 068 4

Printed in Great Britain by
Butler & Tanner Ltd
Frome and London

TO MY WIFE

A MAHOGANY STOOL with saddle seat.
Temp. George II.
(*Collection of Alfred Jowett, Esq.*)

INTRODUCTION

It is instructive to look back nearly fifty years to the publication of Symonds's *Masterpieces of English Furniture and Clocks*. This was a publishing event of some significance—being a limited edition of 1,250 copies and reflecting high standards of plates and general production—standards which were soon to be drastically affected by the economies of the Second World War.

The importance of this book, certainly one of Symonds's best known works, is that it can be read today without any feeling of it being superseded or having to be substantially revised. Symonds with his architectural training had an acute sense of craftsmanship and design coupled with thorough research. He understood the construction of furniture and even more importantly how the craftsman worked. His appreciation of the part played by each type of craftsman, chairmaker or clockmaker—not all 'furniture makers' as so frequently described today—backed up by research into contemporary newspapers and invoices revealed the depth of his knowledge. Above all in his continuing emphasis on the difference between good and bad design (a typical quote in this book is 'over lavish use of ornament') he sought to educate both his own collector clients and the general reader.

The range of subjects covered in this book is very wide, but Symonds showed the same approach in all chapters be it the differences between oriental and European lacquer or the intracacies of clock-making. The chapter on Thomas Tompion was followed some ten years later by his great monograph *Thomas Tompion: His Life and Work*.

Although Symonds wrote articles across the whole field of furniture covering many different centuries, and indeed his last book, published posthumously in 1962 was *Victorian Furniture*, it was in the late 17th and early 18th centuries, the period covered in 'Masterpieces', that he made his mark and it was probably here that he felt most at home.

Robert Symonds had a good relationship with many furniture dealers such as Rob Kern, Sam Wolsey, and my father. According to his daughter Virginia, I came to tea as a very small child to his wartime home at Ripley, just after the publication of 'Masterpieces'. Many of the pieces he advised his clients to purchase came from dealers, but he had a strongly independent mind and would not be influenced against his better judgement. He and the specialist dealers respected each other for the different contributions they made to the understanding of furniture. He was like them a great individualist.

JEROME PHILLIPS
Phillips of Hitchin, July 1986

PREFACE

In this volume I have described certain aspects of design, material and workmanship as applied to old English furniture. By citing from contemporary writings, I have endeavoured to create in the reader's mind a correct picture of the conditions under which the different craftsmen, engaged in furniture-making, were working in the seventeenth and eighteenth centuries. The conditions ruling in these two centuries are reflected often in the quaint wording of a tradesman's announcement, whether it is an advertisement for his wares, a notice of the burning down of his premises, or a bill with the description and the price of an article he had made and sold.

The examples illustrated have been chosen because in the main they exhibit the best as regards design, and quality of material and workmanship. In my selection I have avoided articles of exotic and untraditional character, as I believe that an understanding of furniture comes mainly from the familiarising of the eye with what is good in design and quality, as by this method the defects of the article of poor design and inferior quality are made more obvious.

In a world possessed of so much ugly modern furniture, old English furniture, because of its high standard of design, becomes an important heritage ; it can no longer be treated as the subject of a rich man's hobby.

The chapters on clocks and barometers treat of these articles in the same manner ; design and quality being all-important in their assessment. In this portion of the book I have devoted a chapter to Thomas Tompion, in which I have endeavoured to gather all the available data concerning this eminent master, and in illustrating his consummate skill I have been fortunate in being able to reproduce several outstanding examples of his clocks.

I am indebted to the several owners who have so kindly granted me permission to illustrate their furniture, clocks and barometers, and particularly to Mr. J. S. Sykes, from whose outstanding collection I have chosen numerous examples. To Major Sir John Prestige I am especially grateful, not only for allowing me to include several clocks from his important collection, but also for his most helpful assistance in reading through and revising my text relating to this portion of the work. In this latter connection I have also to thank Mr. Malcolm Webster for information which, from time to time, he has so kindly given me.

R. W. SYMONDS.

29, Bruton Street,
    Berkeley Square, W.1.
March, 1940.

CONTENTS

COLOUR PLATES

A WALNUT PIER TABLE which displays the greatest elegance in form and a
tasteful choice of ornament.   2 ft. in width.   *Temp.* George I.
(*Collection of Geoffrey Blackwell, Esq., O.B.E.*)

CHAPTER I
CHAIR-MAKING IN THE 18TH CENTURY

CHAIRMAKING was a specialised branch of joinery. It was composed of several different trades—the chair-frame-maker who constructed the frame, the carver who executed the carved ornament, and the upholsterer who carried out the stuffing and the covering of the upholstered parts. There was yet one other trade, that of the turner, but this craftsman, who in the 17th century decorated the uprights, legs and stretcher rails of chairs with turning, played in the 18th century a far less important rôle. In this latter century he still retained, however, the monopoly of making kitchen and other cheap varieties of turned chairs.

A chair differs from a bookcase, cabinet or table because it is a movable article, and not being of a uniform design its appearance varies from every angle that it is viewed. These characteristics of a chair were the cause of chairmaking becoming a specialised branch of the joiner's craft. It was specialised to the degree that, as Thomas Sheraton wrote in his *Cabinet Dictionary* (1803) ". . . . those who professedly work at it, seldom engage to make cabinet furniture. In the country manufactories it is otherwise ; yet even these pay some regard to keeping their workmen constantly at the chair, or to the cabinet work." Sheraton also commented on the fact that " The two branches [chair- and cabinet-making] seem evidently to require different talents in workmen, in order to become proficients. In the chair branch it requires a particular turn in the handling of shapes, to make them agreeable and easy : . . . It is very remarkable,"

Fig. 1. A WALNUT DINING CHAIR with compass seat. *Temp.* George I.
(*Collection of Guy N. Charrington, Esq.*)

he goes on to say, "the difference of some chairs of precisely the same pattern, when executed by different chairmakers, arising chiefly in the want of taste concerning the beauty of an outline, of which we judge by the eye, more than the rigid rules of geometry. Drawing, in perspective, seems more proper for those who keep to the cabinet branch, which enables them more accurately to judge of a sketch given them to work by, and of the effect of the whole."

It was this " handling of shapes, to make them agreeable and easy " that caused the craft of the 18th century chairmaker to differ so greatly from that of the cabinet-maker, whose work could be accurately shown in a scale drawing depicting the front and side elevations of a piece of furniture. A chair leg, arm or an upright to a back designed in the form of a three dimensional curve required considerable skill for its proper execution. Therefore, " the beauty of an outline " was greatly dependent upon the " taste " of the craftsman.

The 18th century saw the advent of the chair with its legs, arms, back and seat composed of harmonious curves, *vide* Fig. 3. This type of chair was in contrast to the chair of the 17th century, in which the legs, rails and uprights were straight and of rectangular construction, *vide* Fig. 2. (Chairs of the time of Charles II began to exhibit a curved outline in the arms and front legs.)

From the constructional point of view the chair with straight legs, stretchers and uprights was far more satisfactory, as a curved wooden leg or arm always had a tendency to

1

Fig. 2. A WALNUT CHAIR with frame "turned all-over." *Temp.* Charles II.
(*Courtesy of Messrs. H. M. Lee & Sons.*)

legs, arm and uprights, *vide* Figs. 8, 11 and 12. The variety of mahogany known as Cuban, was found especially suitable for chair construction, as it had a straightness of grain and firmness of texture—two essentials for chair wood.

English chairs of the 18th century have a very long range as regards design and quality. At one end is the example of "London make," constructed from the best quality timber with perfect execution, both as regards the elegant shaping of the component parts and the treatment of the carving. At the other end of the scale is a heavy ungainly chair, lacking all sense of unity and with carved decoration (in many cases over-lavish) of a coarse execution. Such a chair is generally of provincial make.

The country-made chair of the village joiner and turner is not included in these remarks, as it belongs to a different category. Although this chair was generally made of cheap and coarse wood and of rough workmanship, yet its design is nearly always good. The reason is that it owes much more to tradition than the fashionable chair of the town upon which the maker has expended much ingenuity to keep its design up to date.

fracture at those parts where the grain runs out. Wood with its straightness of grain demands a rectangular construction. The 18th century chairmaker, however, tried to overstep this limitation; the unskilled craftsman by making the curved arm, leg or upright unduly thick and heavy; the skilled craftsman by using the finest quality close-grained timber.

The employment of mahogany by the chairmaker soon resulted in chairs becoming lighter in design. It was found that the strength of this new timber permitted the use of open work splats and the reduction in thickness of all constructional members—

The publication in the middle years of the eighteenth century of books of furniture designs, such as those of Chippendale, Ince and Mayhew, and a Society of Upholsterers, and Cabinet-Makers, had a far-reaching effect in standardising furniture design throughout the country. During the first fifty or sixty years of the eighteenth century provincial

Fig. 3. A WALNUT ARMCHAIR with " bended back." The harmonious curves which form the back, arms and front legs
endow it with a particular elegance. *Temp.* George I.
(*Collection of J. S. Sykes, Esq.*)

3

Fig. 4.   AN ARMCHAIR with walnut frame and stuffed back and seat covered with original needlework made specially for the chair.   *Temp.* George I.
(*Collection of J. S. Sykes, Esq.*)

5

furniture of walnut and mahogany possessed varying characteristics of design, according to the district in which it was made. Chairs more than any other type of furniture responded to the influence of local design.

The quality of the execution of provincial chairmaking was on the whole fairly high. What the provincial chairmaker lacked was a sense of design. This was due to his not possessing the same technique of the skilled London craftsman, who achieved elegance of design through fine craftsmanship.

Chairs made in the first half of the 18th century in the northern counties of England — Northumberland, Cumberland, Westmorland, Durham—have certain characteristics of design, such as an attenuated webbed claw foot, round stump back legs, and a shaped front seat rail either plain or decorated with carving.

The example Fig. 6 is a chair of this type; stump back legs, heavy shaped seat rail and workmanship and material of good quality. These North Country examples are very similar in character to contemporary Colonial American chairs, especially those which were made in Pennsylvania.

Fig. 5. A WALNUT SHAVING CHAIR with compass seat. *Temp.* George I
(*Collection of Lord Plender, G.B.E.*)

A constructional feature common to both English chairs of North Country make and Philadelphian chairs is that the tenons of the side rails go right through the member forming the leg and upright of the back. This similarity of design and construction may be accounted for by the emigration in the 18th century of craftsmen from these parts of England to the American colonies.

No actual evidence of this emigration has yet come to light, but it appears the only likely explanation of the connection between the

trade of chair-making as it was practised in the Northern Counties of England and Philadelphian chair-making.

The following excerpts from sale advertisements are of especial interest, as amongst other information, they give the contemporary names of different types of chairs.

At SURMAN'S Great House in Soho-Square, St. Anne's, all the fine Works of the noted Mr. JAMES FAUCON Cabinet-maker and Glass-grinder: . . . several Dozens of the newest fashion'd Wallnut-tree Chairs, cover'd with Velvet, Damask, black Spanish Leather, or uncover'd, fine Mahogony Chairs, Virginia

7

Fig. 6. A MAHOGANY CHAIR of North Country make.
Mid. 18th Century
(*Collection of Alfred Jowett, Esq.*)

Wallnut-tree Chairs with matted Bottoms, Beech Chairs of several Sorts, fine Wallnut-tree Dressing Chairs, Close-stool Chairs, Satees and Chair Beds, . . . (Cf., *The Daily Post*, February 19, 1731.)

. . . the rich Stock in Trade of Mr. ALEXANDER PERRY, an eminent Cabinet-maker, at the Great White House in King Street, Bloomsbury, that End near Holbourn : . . . fine Wallnut-tree and Mahogany Chairs of the newest Fashion, cover'd or uncover'd with Spanish Leather, Damask or Mohair : with other Chairs, from Two Shillings apiece to Forty : several fine Dressing Chairs, Shaving Chairs, Close-stool Chairs and Easy Chairs. (Cf, *The Daily Post*, March 15, 1733.)

From these announcements it would appear that in the second quarter of the 18th century walnut and mahogany were equally favoured for chairs of the newest fashion. The London joiner and turner chair-makers used beech for cheap chairs, but in those country districts where beech trees were not plentiful, English oak and elm were generally employed.

Virginia walnut was imported American walnut ; it was a sound straight-grained timber, and was much in favour with the London cabinet and chair-makers during the first half of the century. Judging from chairs made of this walnut, it would appear that it was sometimes stained and polished so that it would pass as mahogany.

The upholstering of chairs with black Spanish leather, the edges close-nailed with brass-headed nails, was a particularly favoured form of upholstery in the 18th century. Mohair was also another covering material much used by upholsterers. A chair with " a matted bottom " was one with a rush seat.

" Dressing Chairs " were chairs presumably designed for use at a dressing table. Ince and Mayhew in their *Universal System of Houshold Furniture*, illustrate armchairs with fretted backs in the Chinese taste, which they term " Dressing Chairs." A " Shaving " chair was a chair with a high back upon which the head could be supported. Such chairs in the 18th century were corner chairs with the addition of a third splat contained within a cresting rail and uprights fixed to the curved rail of the back. An earlier walnut example with a solid splat as the head rest is illustrated, Fig. 5. A " Close-stool " chair was a chair fitted with

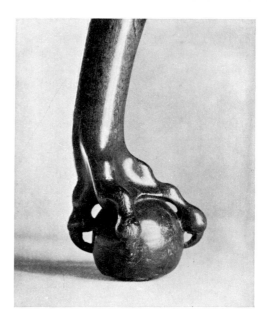

DETAIL of a chair leg showing fine modelling
of Claw Foot of unusual design

PLATE II

AN EASY CHAIR

with walnut frame and original silk needlework covering.   *Temp*. Queen Anne

(Collection of Geoffrey Hart, Esq.)

9

PLATE III

A CHAIR WITH WALNUT FRAME (one of a set of six)
with Mortlake tapestry covering specially worked for the chair frame.   *Temp.* George II (*circa* 1735)
(*Collection of Geoffrey Hart, Esq.*)

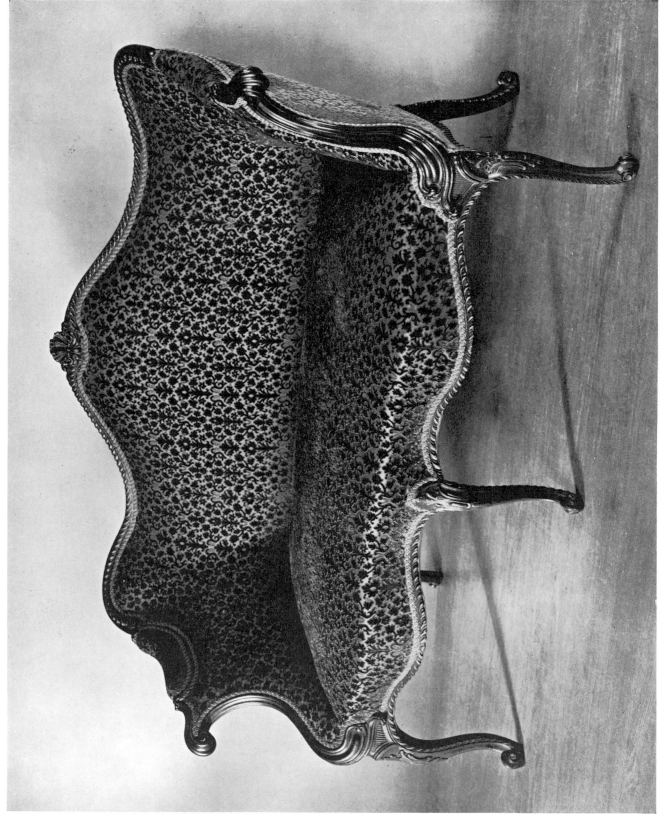

Fig. 7. A COUCH in the French manner. *Temp.*, George III. The repeated use of the serpentine curve has resulted in a composition of unusual character and harmony

(Courtesy of Messrs. M. Harris & Sons)

13

Fig. 8.   A MAHOGANY ARMCHAIR.   The slender uprights and the delicate pierced splat to the back were only made possible through the strength of the timber.   The elegant curves of the arms and legs display the skill of the craftsman.   *Circa* 1760

(*Collection of H. James Yates, Esq.*)

15

Fig. 9. AN ARMCHAIR, in the French manner with mahogany frame, with stuffed back and seat, covered with contemporary needlework. The carving is enriched with gilding. *Circa* 1760.

(*Collection of J. S. Sykes, Esq.*)

17

Fig. 10. AN OVAL STOOL with walnut frame ; the junction of the serpentine stretchers is covered with a leaf. *Temp.*, George I

foot " which had hitherto been so popular. The couch in the French manner, Fig. 7, is an outstanding example of the skill of the chair-maker in " the handling of shapes, to make them agreeable and easy."

The two mahogany chairs, Figs. 11 and 12, which are both dining chairs, show the radical change that took place in chair design between the years 1755 and 1790. The older chair with cabriole legs is the same as a design in Chippendale's *Director* (1st edition, 1754). It is, therefore, highly probable that this chair, together with its five companion chairs (originally there were probably a larger number with two armchairs), came from this maker's workshop in St. Martin's Lane. The quality of the workmanship is too good for this set to be the work of a provincial chair-maker copying the design from Chippendale's plate. The later chair with square back is an outstanding example of the carver's craft ; the ornament on the back being of the most perfect execution.

In the 18th century chairs reached the highest degree of perfection as regards elegance of design and quality of execution. Throughout the centuries the chair's development was a progress from heaviness and coarseness of construction to elegance and refinement ; from a wooden seat relieved by a cushion, to the comfort of a chair with an upholstered seat and back.

a pewter pan and a hinged seat, whilst an easy chair was an armchair with upholstered back fitted with wings to protect the occupant from draughts. The legs of this latter type of chair were short, so as to allow the seat to have a squab cushion which greatly increased the comfort, *vide* Frontispiece and colour plate II.

An innovation in chair design that took place in the reign of Queen Anne was that the backs of chairs, hitherto designed with caned panels, were now fitted with veneered splats. The silhouette of the splats was in the form of a vase or baluster. Another novel design of this period was the shaping of the back of a chair to accommodate the back of the occupant, *vide* Figs. 1 and 3. This feature, which at the time was called a " bended back," was much in vogue in the reign of George I. Chairs with " bended backs " often possessed " Compass seats " which were, as the name implies, round seats, *vide* Fig. 1. Such chairs were termed " compass chairs " ; they were particularly fashionable between the years 1715 and 1730.

From 1740 to 1750 chair design, like all other branches of the crafts, was affected by the French style. Cabriole legs now terminated in the French scroll toe instead of the " claw

Fig. 10A. A WALNUT STOOL with turned legs and stretchers. *Temp.*, George I
(*Collection of J. S. Sykes, Esq.*)

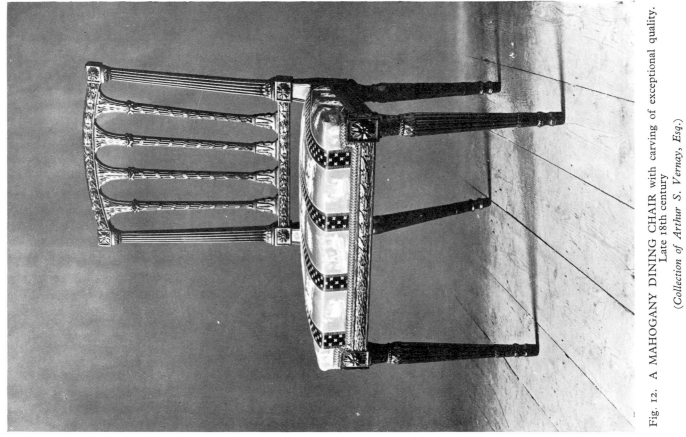

Fig. 12. A MAHOGANY DINING CHAIR with carving of exceptional quality.
Late 18th century

(Collection of Arthur S. Vernay, Esq.)

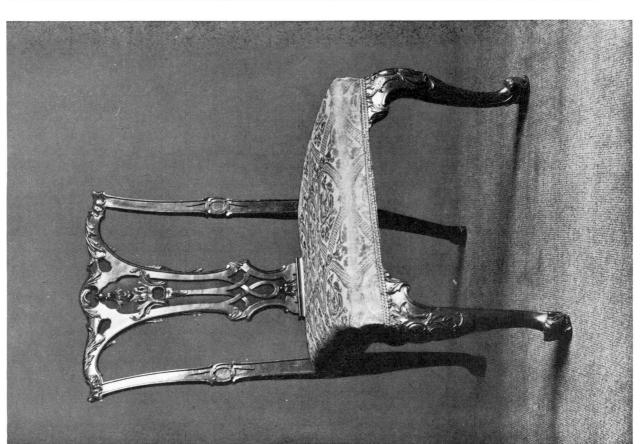

Fig. 11. A MAHOGANY DINING CHAIR, probably made by Thomas
Chippendale, being of *Director* design and of the highest quality

(Collection of the late Francis P. Garvan, Esq)

20

Fig. 13. MAHOGANY CANDLESTANDS in the Chinese taste, possibly made by William Hallett of Cannons for Sir Jacob
Bouverie. Mid-18th Century

(Collection of the Earl of Radnor)

22

CHAPTER II
THE QUALITY AND DESIGN OF MAHOGANY FURNITURE

THE craftsmanship and material of eighteenth century mahogany furniture varied in quality to a considerable degree. The furniture of the finest quality was the work of cabinet-makers who were patronized by the aristocracy and the wealthy classes. In the construction of this furniture the best quality timber and the finest figured veneers were used, and cabinet-makers, joiners and carvers, who were highly skilled in their crafts, were employed. The majority of this fine quality and expensive furniture was made by London and not by provincial craftsmen.

The London trade of cabinet-making was by no means confined to firms of the first rank; both in the Cities of London and Westminster as well as the suburbs very many master cabinet-makers in a small way of business were producing mahogany furniture of good quality to suit the requirements of the middle classes. In comparison with the furniture of the highest quality, the design of this latter kind of furniture was, generally speaking, more simple and the carving, which was used sparingly, was not of the same high standard. The mahogany veneers lacked the fine mottled figuring and were accordingly cheaper, and neither the cabinet-work nor the polishing possessed the high technical finish that characterized the furniture of the first grade. By the last half of the eighteenth century the production of this second-grade mahogany furniture must have considerably increased in London to fulfil the wants of a much larger middle class. The making of first-grade furniture did not increase, however, to the same

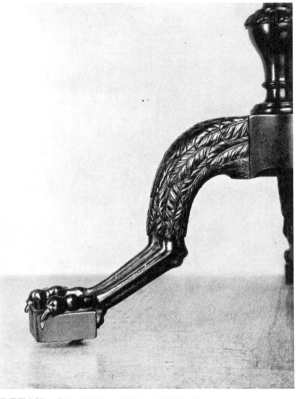

DETAIL OF LEG OF A FIRESCREEN. (Fig. 15.)
Temp. George II
(*Collection of J. S. Sykes, Esq.*)

extent as that of the second grade, as the wealthy upper classes were not multiplying in the same ratio. Another factor that restricted the production of mahogany of the first grade was the vogue for satinwood.

In the last half of the eighteenth century in the large provincial towns the production of mahogany furniture must also have been considerable.

In the first half of the eighteenth century provincial chair-and-cabinet-makers made their best furniture mostly of walnut, except perhaps in such seaport towns as Bristol, Liverpool and Plymouth, where mahogany timber was shipped direct from Jamaica. This fact accounts for the large amount of Georgian walnut furniture that has survived. Even in London, between the years 1725 and 1750, the production of walnut furniture must have been in excess of mahogany. In cabinet-makers' advertisements of this period the mention of furniture made either of "walnut-tree or mahogany" was a common feature, thus showing that the new mahogany wood had at this time by no means supplanted the walnut.

As the production of mahogany furniture increased in the late eighteenth century the standard of its quality became lower. This was the inevitable result of enlarging the market for mahogany until it became in general use and was no longer restricted to the making of good quality furniture for the well-to-do. This reduction in quality was brought about by the sparing use of mahogany and the employment of cheap soft woods for carcasses and drawer linings instead of more expensive hard woods.

23

Fig. 14. A MAHOGANY CANDLESTAND of
graceful form, one of a pair. Mid-18th Century
(Courtesy of J. M. Botibol, Esq.)

The tops of sideboards, tables and chests-of-drawers were veneered on a deal carcass and drawer linings and interiors of bookcases and cupboards were of deal instead of the more costly oak or mahogany as in the better quality furniture.

These economic factors concerning eighteenth-century mahogany furniture are reflected in the percentage of it that is extant to-day. Pieces of the finest quality are extremely rare, pieces of the more ordinary or simple type of good quality material and sound craftsmanship are fairly common, and the cheap grade mahogany furniture, the majority of which dates approximately from 1780 to Victorian times, exists in considerable quantities.

A distinguishing feature of mahogany of the first grade from that of the second, apart from quality, is the difference in scale. The rooms in the " edifices " and mansions of the aristocracy and wealthy were planned to a far larger scale than the rooms in the " common house," which was furnished with furniture of the second grade and lived in by tenants who possessed moderate incomes.

For apartments of spacious and lofty proportions, articles of furniture were designed of large and tall dimensions so as to be in harmony of scale with their surroundings. It is for this reason that the majority of mahogany bookcases, writing- dining- and side-tables, commodes and looking-glasses, and suites consisting of couches, chairs and stools, when of the first grade, are of large dimensions. The chairs that were designed for the " best Dineing Room " in a nobleman's house were larger than the chairs used in the dining-parlours of the middle classes, being several inches wider and deeper in the seat and higher in the back.

The wealthy aristocracy called upon the London cabinet-maker and upholsterer to supply the furniture and upholstery for their country mansions. The provincial tradesman was not in the position as regards skilled labour, nor was his furniture fashionable enough in design, to allow him to carry out an important commission of this kind. The fashionable London chair- and cabinet-makers, upholsterers, japanners, carvers and gilders had their shops and warehouses (*i.e.*, workshops) in the neighbourhood of Long Acre, St. Martin's Lane and the Strand, *vide* Fig. 36. Tradesmen of

Fig. 15. A FIRESCREEN with needlework panel on pillar and claw. Temp. George II. For detail
of the unusual foot see page 23

Collection of J. S. Sykes, Esq.

Fig. 17. A MAHOGANY KETTLE-STAND with scroll legs of a rare design.
Mid-18th Century
(Collection of Lord Plender, G.B.E.)

Fig. 16. A MAHOGANY KETTLE-STAND with hexagonal galleried top and
fluted pillar. Mid-18th Century
(Collection of J. S. Sykes, Esq.)

lesser standing resided in the City, St. Paul's Churchyard, around Holborn and Clerkenwell and other suburbs, also Southwark south of the river.

To consider in more detail some of the furniture of the mahogany period, a particularly favoured variety of table was one with a tripod foot. The tripod support was used extensively by London and provincial cabinet-makers and joiners for tables, kettle- and candle-stands, dumb-waiters and also fire-screens. Its age-long popularity was due to the particular merit of stability that it possessed owing to the three legs being able to stand firmly on an uneven floor.

The tripod table and stand were the product of three craftsmen ; the carver who shaped the legs and enhanced the piece with ornament ; the turner who turned the pillar and top, and the joiner who assembled together the top, the pillar and the legs.

The mahogany tripod table was made in tens of thousands in all grades of quality from the best to the poorest. The reason for it being in so great demand was its general usefulness as a table for all purposes and the ease with which it could be moved about. By far the larger number were unadorned with carving, the top being constructed of a plain slab of mahogany and the only ornamentation being the pillar with its turned members and sometimes with a gadrooned bulb. Such plain examples must have been widely used in all classes of dwellings, including taverns, coffee houses and also tea gardens. The cheaper tripod tables were of oak but this type has survived in fewer numbers, perhaps for the reason that they were not so well made and their tops were usually joined ; in consequence they were not able to withstand wear and tear to the same degree as the stronger examples made in mahogany. The mahogany tripod table nearly always —in fact one might say invariably—had the top constructed of one piece of timber.

The tripod table made of good quality, close-grained mahogany, with the legs of an elegant curve decorated with well-executed carving, and with the top carved with a pie-crust edge, was usually the product of the London cabinet-maker. The contemporary name for such a table was a " claw table " or a table " with a pillar and claw." The term " claw " referred to the eagle's claw, which was the carver's favourite motif for ornamenting

Fig. 18. A MAHOGANY KETTLE-STAND
with turned pillar. *Temp. George II*
(*Collection of J. S. Sykes, Esq.*)

the feet (*vide* Figs. 16, 19). The eagle's leg and claw forming the feet of the tripod of a fire-screen (Fig. 15) is an exceptional example of the employment of this eagle motif. In fact the present writer knows only of one other tripod of similar design belonging to a dumb-waiter.[1]

As evidence of the variation in quality of claw tables, Thos. Bullas supplied in 1745 to Lord Strafford " A pillar & Claw table " for the sum of twelve shillings. Benjamin Goodison between the years 1729 and 1733 supplied the Royal Wardrobe with numerous claw tables at prices ranging from 35s. to 50s. Such tables must have been of superior quality, and, perhaps, of a more elaborate design than Lord Strafford's table. The outstanding example of a claw table, illustrated Fig. 19, was probably of the quality of those supplied by Goodison. The example with scroll legs, Fig. 21, is also another table of exceptional quality as regards execution and material.

The kettle stand, a smaller edition of the tripod table, was designed to support the kettle, and stood beside the tea table.

The examples illustrated show three alternative tripod designs. The stand, Fig. 16, has the most usual construction, each leg being fixed to the base of the pillar by a dovetailed

[1] *Cf., English Furniture from Charles II to George II.* R. W. Symonds, 1929.

PLATE IV

A MAHOGANY FRAME CHAIR

with arm terminals decorated with lion heads ; the back and seat are covered with contemporary needlework

Temp. George II

(*Collection of J. S. Sykes, Esq.*)

Figs. 19 and 20. A MAHOGANY TABLE with turned and carved pillar and legs terminating in claw and ball feet. The top is carved with a gadrooned pie-crust edge decorated with shells. Mid-18th century

(Collection of Lord Plender, G.B.E.)

Figs. 21 and 22. A MAHOGANY TABLE with carved pillar and scroll legs of a rare design. *Temp.* Mid-18th century
(*Collection of J. S. Sykes, Esq.*)

32

Fig. 23. A MAHOGANY CARD-TABLE. The form of the cabriole legs is unusually graceful and the carving
is of high quality. *Temp.* Mid-18th century

(*Collection of J. S. Sykes, Esq.*)

joint. The stand, Fig. 17, with scroll legs is of a rare design and few examples of this type are extant. The plain example, Fig. 18, shows an alternative construction of the tripod in which the pillar is fixed by being screwed into a platform upheld by the legs.

The stand, Fig. 14, was designed to hold a candlestick. It was an article that enjoyed considerable popularity from the time of Charles II to the beginning of the reign of George III. Up to the reign of George I it was made usually as part of a suite, which consisted of two stands, a dressing-table and a looking-glass (*vide* page 61). The later walnut and mahogany stands appear, however, to have been made independently of the table

and looking-glass, and were now used to support a light that could be easily moved about a room for reading or writing. Elizabeth Gumley and William Turing, cabinet-makers, supplied to the Royal Wardrobe in 1727 " a fine Walnuttree Bureau Table & Stands, £8 10s." The stands which flanked the bureau illuminated it for writing. Many mahogany candle-stands have survived in pairs, which suggests that the cabinet-makers did not make them singly.

By virtue of the fine quality of their material and workmanship, the five pieces of furniture, illustrated in Figs. 24 to 29, can be identified as the work of London cabinet-makers of the first rank.

Fig. 24. THE MAHOGANY PEDESTAL WRITING TABLE (illustrated Fig. 25), showing the side fitted
with cupboards and drawers

From its design the writing table, Figs, 24 and 25, dates about the middle years of the 18th century. The lavish use of the " rose and ribbon " motif decorating the mouldings which surround the plain unbeaded drawer fronts, and the circular panels on the ends of the desk formed by applied mouldings (also carved with " rose and ribbon "), denote that this desk does not belong to the Chippendale school of design. There are extant a few mahogany writing tables and commodes which have similar characteristics to this desk, but none of these pieces has so far been identified as the work of any particular cabinet-maker. Perhaps one day the discovery of an example with its original bill will enable the identification to take place.

The commode, Fig. 26, with shaped front supported on paw feet, also does not bear the imprint of Chippendale's design. In its general character it possesses a similarity to the furniture in Chippendale's *Director*, but this is due to the *Director* designs being of the same contemporary style. In the book of furniture designs by a Society of Upholsterers, Cabinet-Makers (*circa* 1760) there is a commode which has a strong resemblance to the one under review, in fact, far more so, than any example in the three editions of the *Director*.

This commode is a part of a set of drawing room furniture consisting of two commodes and two pier glasses. The frames of the glasses are of rococo design with masks, birds, rams' heads and flowers. The carving and gilding of the frames exhibit the same fine quality of workmanship as that of the commodes, due to both commodes and glasses emanating from the same workshop. [1]

---

[1] When these commodes and the companion pier glasses were sold recently by auction, the commodes became divorced from the glasses ; the breaking-up of this interesting suite of furniture is much to be regretted.

Fig. 25. A MAHOGANY PEDESTAL WRITING TABLE of exceptional quality. A view of the opposite side fitted with cupboards is shown in Fig. 24. This table was one of the furnishing items of Temple Newsum, Yorks, in the mid. 18th century

(*Collection of G. Huntingdon Hartford, Esq.*)

35

Fig. 26. A MAHOGANY COMMODE with cupboard doors designed with dummy drawer fronts. *Circa* 1760. This commode and its companion with pier glasses *en suite* were a part of the 18th century furnishing of Hampden House, Buckinghamshire, the seat of the Earl of Buckinghamshire.

(Courtesy of Messrs. Frank Partridge & Sons)

37

Fig. 27. A "CHINA TABLE" of Ince and Mayhew's design and probably from the workshop of this celebrated firm of cabinet-makers. *Circa* 1760. This piece of furniture was designed for the purpose of displaying china
(Collection of Geoffrey Blackwell, Esq., O.B.E.)

39

Fig. 28. A COMMODE of serpentine form. Mid-18th century. The design and quality of this example suggest the work of Thomas Chippendale

41

Fig. 29.   A MAHOGANY COMMODE DRESSING TABLE with fitted top drawer. *Circa* 1760
Several designs of Commode Dressing Tables are shown in Chippendale's *Director*
(*Collection of Lord Plender, G.B.E.*)

Fig. 30.   A MAHOGANY CARD TABLE with legs of an elegant form terminating in claw feet.   Mid-18th century.
(*Collection of J. S. Sykes, Esq.*)

Fig. 31. A SIDEBOARD TABLE with mahogany frame. The carved motif of a bunch of grapes signifying wine is appropriate for a table used in the dining room. *Temp.* George II. (This table is an example of the incorrectness of employing a console as a table leg, a practice which was introduced in the second quarter of the 18th century by architect furniture designers such as William Kent.)

(*Collection of J. S. Sykes, Esq.*)

Ince and Mayhew's *Universal System of Houshold Furniture* contains a plate entitled " China Table and Shelf " which is very similar in design to the piece illustrated in Fig. 27. In Ince and Mayhew's plate the table is depicted surmounted by a tier of open shelves for the display of china, and instead of bracket feet as belong to the illustrated example the plate shows the table supported on short legs. If the table illustrated was not made in the designers' own workshop, its design assuredly originated from the book. The former assumption would appear the more likely owing to the quality of the execution ; a cabinet-maker who could produce furniture of this high standard would be unlikely to copy a competitor's illustrated design. This piece of furniture, as its name implied, was designed for the display of china, which even when placed behind the open fret doors of the two cupboards would still be visible.

The fact that the design of this china table can be attributed to Ince and Mayhew shows how erroneous is the present-day habit of collectors and dealers in naming all furniture designed in the Chinese taste — " Chinese Chippendale."

The commode, Fig. 28, with its serpentine

Fig 32. A MAHOGANY LONG-CASE CLOCK with tapering case partaking of pedestal design, the movement by John Holmes, London

(*In the Pennsylvania Museum, Philadelphia, U.S.A.*)

front and carved trusses decorating the canted corners, is an example that is more characteristic of Thomas Chippendale's design than any of the three preceding pieces. The subtle curve of the serpentine shape, the design of the trusses and the quality both of the carving and the execution of the cabinet work are all features peculiar to Chippendale's technique.

The mahogany case of the clock, Figs 32 and 32A, designed in the form of a pedestal, is of a type that was but occasionally made in the middle years of the 18th century. It also does not follow the traditional design of contemporary clock-cases and would appear therefore to be the product of the cabinet-maker rather than the case-maker.[1] The latter craftsman, who by trade was a cabinet-maker, specialised in the making of clock cases; other case-makers also confined their work to the production of cases for musical instruments.[2] The trade card of a clock-case-maker is illustrated on page 171.

[1] In Chippendale's *Director* there is a design of a clock-case in the form of a tapering pedestal of a similar type to the clock illustrated.

[2] The term " Casemaker " appears occasionally in the Clockmakers' Company's records; this craftsman, however, was a watch-case-maker and a worker in metal. The clock-case-maker being a worker in wood was not eligible to the Clockmakers' Company.

Fig. 32A. DETAIL of hood of long-case clock illustrated in Fig. 32

It would appear that the occasional clock-case—usually a special order—made by the cabinet-maker was invariably executed in mahogany and displayed a lavish use of carving similar to the examples depicted in Chippendale's *Director*. A table clock-case which was made by " John Bradburn," cabinet-maker, for Queen Charlotte's bedchamber at the Queen's House in St. James's Park, is an example of a cabinet-maker's clock-case.

For a Mohogany Comode shaped Clock Case with a plate Glass Door in front and a neat joint handle at Top, £5-15.

¹ The clock-case-makers of Lancashire and Cheshire in the late 18th and early 19th centuries made a type of mahogany case decorated with carved mouldings and Chinese and Gothic frets ; many long-case clocks with this type of highly decorated case are extant.

The case-maker, unlike the cabinet-maker, seldom used carving[1]—he was particularly skilled in the making of pierced fret—and continued to employ walnut for the cases of long-case clocks until past the middle of the 18th century. He also continued to make japanned-cases for long-case clocks after japanned furniture had declined in fashion *vide* p. 90. The japan work of these late cases was of inferior quality, and the examples that have survived—mostly with the dark grounds black, blue and green—are only a percentage of the original production.

In design also the case-maker had a conservative taste, as many clocks, barometers and spinets, dating as late as 1760, have walnut veneered cases of a style that belongs to several decades earlier.

From the remarks contained in this and the previous chapter it will be gathered that in the 17th and 18th centuries there was no such individual as a " furniture maker." Furniture was made by a number of individual craftsmen, each a specialist in a particular branch. There were chair- and cabinet-makers, joiners and turners, carvers and japanners, gilders, upholsterers and case-makers.

In the 18th century the cabinet-maker often combined with the upholsterer and these two tradesmen employed journeymen of all the subsidiary trades, so that the partnership could supply the complete furniture of a house as well as the carpets, curtains and linen.

In some cases cabinet-makers were more shop-keepers than makers.

" Many of their Shops [cabinet-makers'] are so richly set out that they look more like Palaces, and their Stocks are of exceeding great Value. But this Business seems to consist, as do many others, of two Branches, the *Maker* and the *Vender*; for the Shop-keeper does not always make every Sort of Goods that he deals in, though he bears away the Title."

(Cf., *A General Description of all Trades.* 1747.)

A few ambitious cabinet-makers published books of design depicting fashionable furniture as a means of advertisement ; the names of such tradesmen have become household words.

Fig. 33.   A MAHOGANY CABINET made by William Vile for King George III for the refurnishing of St. James's
Palace between the years 1760 and 1764
(*Collection of Geoffrey Blackwell, Esq., O.B.E.*)

CHAPTER III
A ROYAL CABINET BY WILLIAM VILE

DETAIL of Cabinet showing the exceptional quality of the carved ornament to the pediment and cornice

THE beautiful cabinet, the subject of this chapter, is one of several surviving pieces of mahogany furniture that are known to have been made by the cabinet-maker, William Vile. All the examples of William Vile's furniture that are extant were made to the order of King George III, and a large winged bookcase, a secretaire, and a jewel cabinet are still in Royal possession at Buckingham Palace.

The cabinet here illustrated was given by King George III to his youngest child, the Princess Amelia (1783–1810). According to tradition, two other cabinets by Vile also left the possession of the Crown, when King George IV gave them to an Admiral Vavasseur of the Italian navy.[1]

William Vile is recognised as the maker of this group of furniture because the examples at Buckingham Palace are identifiable from the descriptions in Vile's original bills preserved in the Royal Wardrobe Accounts.[2]

The design and the quality of the material and workmanship, endow Vile's furniture with a distinct character, in fact, so much is this the case, that each piece possesses, as it were, the same handwriting.

The " oval of laurels " was a favourite motif of this maker ; in the cabinet illustrated it decorates the central panel of the base. The unusual method of ornamenting the ends of a cabinet with applied panel mouldings was another peculiarity, *vide* Fig. 34, and the employment of veneers of highly figured flash

---

[1] *Old Labelled Furniture*. R. W. Symonds. Art. *Connoisseur*. v. 86.

[2] *Buckingham Palace*. H. Clifford Smith. Country Life Ltd. 1931.

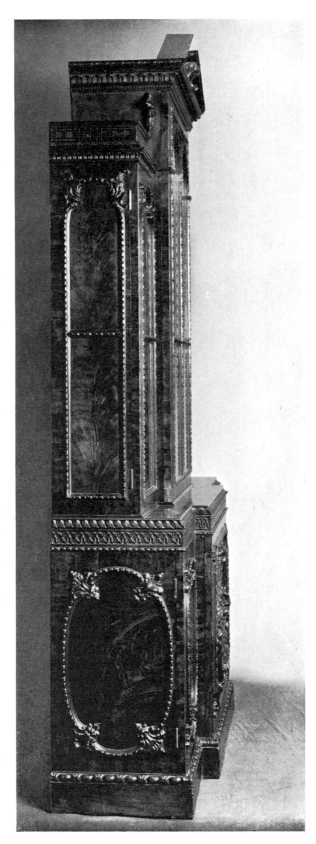

Fig. 34. DETAIL of side of cabinet showing the figured veneer and applied carved mouldings

mahogany and the most perfect finish to the cabinet-work were further distinctive features of this remarkable furniture. The wood carvers employed by Vile must have been the most highly skilled in the trade of their time; the present writer has not seen any carving in mahogany that surpasses that of the cabinet under review.

In one of Vile's numerous bills in the Royal Wardrobe Accounts, there appears the following item for a " Glass Case " supplied for the Passage Room at St. James's Palace.

" For an Exceeding Neat Mohogany Glass Case with Plate Glass Doors at Top and Wood Doors at Bottom Carved Exceeding Rich and neat & Exquisite fine wood all the Backs and Shelves of Mahogany very fine locks and three Keys two of them pearsed & Engraved in a very neat Manner.   £100."

The cabinet answers so closely to this description that it seems highly probable that this item was the actual charge for the cabinet. The backs and shelves are of mahogany, but the two elaborate keys no longer exist. The price of £100, like many of Vile's charges in the Royal Wardrobe Accounts, appears excessive, especially when the purchasing value of money in the middle years of the 18th century is compared with the value at the present time.

In addition to this Royal furniture, it is probably that other pieces of Vile's work are extant, but unidentified, for the reason that they are plainer and less " rich " in design, being examples of a more utilitarian character.

The following notes give all the information concerning William Vile that the author has been able to gather.

An interesting fact is Vile's association with two other eminent cabinet-makers, John Cobb and William Hallett. The former was Vile's partner, and the latter presumably a valued friend, as Vile in his will appointed Hallett one of his executors.

During the first few years of George III's reign, Vile held the Royal Warrant as cabinet-maker to the Crown. During the last fifteen years of his active life he was in partnership with John Cobb, who was by trade an upholsterer. Vile and Cobb's " Cabinet and Upholstery Warehouse " was on the corner of St. Martin's Lane and Long Acre, *vide* Fig. 36. According to the rate books, " William Vile and Co. first paid rates in St. Martin's Lane in the year 1751. In the rate books four entries are made, indicating that the premises occupied were extensive, being either four houses or four properties rated separately. A part of the premises Vile used as his dwelling house. Several facts concerning the partnership with Cobb can be deduced from the following passage in Vile's will, which was written in 1763.

" And Whereas For many years past I have been and now am engaged with my Copartner John Cobb in very Extensive Branches of Trade and not having lately made any Rest of Stock whereby to Enable me to Judge with any Certainty of the Totall Value of my Estate and Effects. . . ."

Vile empowered his two executors, William Hallett of Cannons, and his friend Charles Smith of Portugal Street, upholsterer and cabinet-maker, to adjust and settle all the accounts between himself and Cobb. Vile apparently retired from business before his death in August, 1767, as in an affidavit attached to the will he is described as " formerly of the Parish of Saint Martins in the Fields . . . but late of the Parish of Battersea." It is therefore likely that Vile, in 1763, when he drew up his will, feeling ill in health, and becoming anxious about his financial interests in his partnership with Cobb, decided to straighten out his affairs. Vile's bills no longer appear in the Royal Wardrobe Accounts after

Fig. 35. DETAIL of central cupboard in base of cabinet, showing the superb execution of the carving and the fine figured mahogany veneer

1764-5, which suggests that his active interest in the partnership ceased at this date.

Cobb's name in the Royal Wardrobe Accounts only appears in connection with Vile's, and Cobb's appointment to the Crown appears to have terminated with that of Vile. Many of Vile's bills, however, are rendered in his name alone, and in such cases he is described as a cabinet-maker. He supplied for St. James's Palace and the Queen's House in the Park[1] all types of furniture, ranging from bookcases and wardrobes to a " Flaped Table for the Queen to Breakfast off." His furniture did not, however, include chairs, as Vile was not a chair-maker. The bills of " William Vile and John Cobb Upholsters " rendered jointly are for Wilton and Turkey carpets, curtains, linen and upholstery work.

It is interesting to note that they charged for upholstering the frames of a set of " 8 Mahogany Elbow Chairs with Hollow Seats " supplied to the Royal Wardrobe by Katherine Naish, joiner and chairmaker to the Crown. The charge for the upholstery work, which consisted of "Quilted Welted and bordered & finished Compleat with Burnished Nails . . ." was 51s. per chair, whereas the chair-maker's charge for each chair was only 27s. A few bills, headed " Vile and Cobb Cabinet Makers ", charging several pieces of furniture and mahogany and brass lanterns with their accompanying brass candlesticks, are also preserved in the Royal Wardrobe Accounts.

Unquestionably Vile and Cobb had a large and flourishing

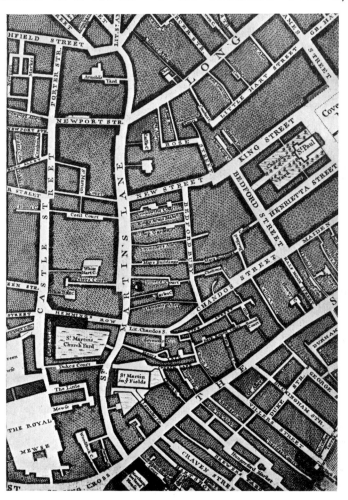

Fig. 36. A SECTION OF THE MAP OF LONDON AND WESTMINSTER made by John Roque ; showing St. Martin's Lane and the adjacent streets in 1747

business and numbered amongst their patrons many members of the nobility. Records exist that they supplied furniture to Horace Walpole for Strawberry Hill between the years 1760–5[2] and also to Richard Chauncey for his house, Edgecote, in Northamptonshire, in 1758.[3] Cobb's name, as already mentioned, no longer appeared in the Royal Wardrobe Accounts after the death of Vile. The cabinet-maker who succeeded to the royal appointment held by Vile was " John Bradburn," who, it would seem, was the same person as the John Bradborn to whom Vile bequeathed a sum of £20, and who, in a codicil to Vile's will, is referred to as one of the testator's servants. Bradborn, presumably, was Vile's foreman cabinet-maker, and he was appointed cabinet-maker to the Crown in place of his deceased master. "John Bradburn" moved into premises in Long Acre in 1767 (the year of Vile's death), where he remained until 1776, when he retired from business. He died at Wandsworth on October 6th, 1781.

On the retirement or death of Vile, Cobb still continued in business at the same address ; in fact, according to the rate books he soon became the occupier of two further houses adjacent to the original four. He also carried on the cabinet-making branch of the business. At Corsham Court, Wiltshire, there is a commode which Cobb made for Paul Methuen in

[1] The Queen's House was originally Buckingham House, which was built in 1705 by John, Duke of Buckingham. In 1762 King George III bought Buckingham House as a dower house for Queen Charlotte. In 1825 King George IV began to build on the site the present Buckingham Palace.

[2] *Strawberry Hill Accounts,* published by Dr. Paget Toynbee in 1927.

[3] *Edgecote.* H. Avray Tipping. *Country Life.* v. 47.

1772. Cobb's original bill, which has also survived, describes this piece of furniture as " an Extra neat Inlaid Comode wth a scaliole Top, wth brass Ornaments £63-5."[1]

In J. T. Smith's work, *Nollekins and his Times*, are found several paragraphs concerning John Cobb.

" The corner house of Long-acre, now No. 72, formed a small part of the extensive premises formerly occupied by that singularly haughty character, Cobb, the Upholsterer, who occasionally employed Banks, the Cellaret-maker, to whom I applied for information respecting him. Cobb, he said, was perhaps one of the proudest men in England; and always appeared in full dress of the most superb and costly kind, in which state he would strut through his workshops, giving orders to his men. He was the person who brought that very convenient table into fashion that draws out in front, with upper and inward rising desks, so healthy for those who stand to write, read, or draw. The late King frequently employed him and often smiled at his pomposity. One day, when Mr. Cobb was in his Majesty's Library at Buckingham-house, giving orders to a workman, whose ladder was placed before a book which the King wanted, his Majesty desired Cobb to hand him the work, which instead of obeying, he called to his man, 'Fellow, give me that book!' The King, with his usual condescension, arose, and asked Cobb what his man's name was. 'Jenkins,' answered the astonished Upholsterer. 'Then,' observed the King, 'Jenkins, you shall hand me the book.' "

*   *   *

" The late Sir Nathaniel Dance Holland, when he was a Portrait-painter, in Tavistock-row, Covent-garden, considered Cobb's tables so useful, that he easily prevailed upon the adonised Upholsterer, to allow him to paint his portrait for one; which picture, after it had remained in Cobb's showroom for some time, purposely to be serviceable, as he said, to the 'poor painter,' he conveyed, in his own carriage, to his seat at Highgate."

John Cobb died on August 24th, 1778, and according to his will he had grown rich by his trade. He had a dwelling house in St. Martin's Lane and also a country residence at Highgate, and another house at Islington. He left to his wife, apart from his " Chariot and Horses," the interest on a capital sum of twenty thousand pounds which was invested in the " two three p^r cent Stocks." The capital and interest after his wife's death were to go to the " now infant Boy William Cobb the Grandson of William Cobb at Mallingford in Norfolk " and his heirs, so as " to support ye Name of Cobb as a private Gentleman."

Cobb's widow, five years after her husband's death, married a Mr. Dinwoodie. In a notice of her marriage she is described as " relict of Mr. C. an eminent cabinet-maker in St. Martin's-lane, and formerly partner with the late Mr. Hallet of Cannons."[2] Apart from this notice no other evidence exists of this partnership between Cobb and Hallet; a possible solution is that they worked sometimes in partnership on a particular contract, which would appear to have been a not unusual procedure with tradesmen in the 18th century.

William Hallett (1707–1782) is an obscure figure in the annals of English cabinet-making. Very little evidence has survived of his activities as an " eminent cabinet-maker." His contemporaries appear to have thought his one claim to fame was that he purchased Cannons, the estate of the Duke of Chandos. The ducal mansion was demolished in 1747, and Hallet purchased by auction some of the building materials, with which he built a villa on the central vaults of the former house.

That he was an exponent of *Chinoiserie* is implied by Horace Walpole, who in one of his letters, when describing a house belonging to a friend, writes, " and the house has undergone Batty Langley discipline: half the ornaments are of his bastard Gothic, and half of Hallett's mongrel Chinese."

There is no known piece of furniture that can be identified as coming from Hallett's workshop. It is possible, however, that the candlestands, Fig. 13, are his work. The following are the reasons for this assumption. Hallett's name appears in the account books of Sir Jacob Bouverie at Longford Castle (Sir Jacob being the first Viscount Folkestone).[3] These candlestands have been at Longford Castle ever since the 18th century, and are undoubtedly an item of furniture that dates back to Sir Jacob Bouverie's time. Because of this and also the fact that they are in the Chinese taste makes it tempting to suggest that they were one of the items of furniture supplied by Hallett.

The following news item recalls a long-forgotten incident, and also mentions Hallett's address in Newport Street (*vide* Fig. 36), where he had premises during the years 1732

---

[1] Cf. *Documented Furniture at Corsham*, Oliver Brackett. Art. *Country Life*, Nov. 28, 1936.

[2] Cf. *The Gentleman's Magazine*, Sept. 6, 1783.

[3] *Furniture at Longford Castle*. Art. *Country Life*, December 12th, 1931.

to 1753. He then moved to Long Acre, where the rate books record his occupation during the years 1753 to 1769.

"On Sunday Night last, as Mr. Hallett and his Wife, an eminent Cabinet-maker, in Newport Street, were returning from Twickenham in a Chaise, in the Dusk of the Evening, they were attack'd by a single Highwayman well mounted, near Kensington-Gore, who bid him deliver, but he not readily complying drove on; he fired at them which graz'd the Top of the Chaise, but he luckily giving the Horse Rein enough, they got off without being Robbed." (Cf., *General Advertiser*, March 5th, 1746–7.)

Evidence of the high respect in which Hallet was held is contained in an advertisement inserted in a New York newspaper in 1771 by a journeyman who was once in his employ.

"Eleven years foreman to the great and eminent cabinet maker, William Hallett, Esq. that bought the fine estate of the Duke of Chandos called Cannons in Middlesex."

Hallet must have been a man of considerable affluence according to the legacies in his will. His son, William Hallett (II) having predeceased him, he left his estate to his grandson, William Hallett [III], who was portrayed by Thomas Gainsborough in the famous picture "A Morning Walk."

That Hallett was a man of commendable character is indicated by Vile in his will, when he states: "I having the greatest opinion of the Honour ability and Integrity of William Hallett of Cannons."

These three craftsmen, William Vile, John Cobb and William Hallett, must have been in their day three of the most eminent members of the London craft of cabinet-making. Unlike others of their trade, they were craftsmen and not shop-keepers, as the majority of the things they sold they made. Their furniture was hall-marked, not only by the quality of the material used in its production—the best Archangel deal or straight-grained mahogany for carcasses, the finest figured veneers and the best wainscot from Riga and Dantzig for the drawer linings—but by the superior quality of the execution of the general cabinet-work, the carving, the inlaying, the polishing, and the mercurial gilding of the metal work.

A PORTRAIT GROUP representing William Hallett (I) with his wife, her parents and his son William Hallett (II) and daughter-in-law and grandchild William Hallett (III), by Francis Hayman, R.A.

Fig. 37.　A WALNUT AND GILT LOOKING-GLASS of architectural design.　*Temp.* George I
(Collection of Lord Plender, G.B E)

CHAPTER IV
THE TRADE OF THE LOOKING-GLASS MAKER

THE looking-glass derived its name by the first looking-glasses being described as "Glasses to loke in." Cardinal Wolsey owned three "Of the seide Glasses at Hampton Courte."

By the end of the reign of Charles II the making of looking-glasses in England had become an accepted and distinct craft. They were made and sold by a specialist in the art, who described himself after his occupation and whose shop often bore the appropriate sign of a looking-glass. Samuel Pepys in his *Diary* states that he bought a looking-glass for five guineas, and that it was delivered home by "the Looking-glass man."

The looking-glass in the seventeenth century was a luxury found only in the mansions of the nobility and the houses of well-to-do citizens, while in the next century, as a contrast, it was in every tradesman's home.

The trades of looking-glass and cabinet-making were frequently combined; a master cabinet-maker took into his employ the various craftsmen who produced the looking-glass plate and its frame. These craftsmen were of several distinct trades, the glass-grinder, who attended to the looking-glass plates, and the joiner, carver and gilder, who produced between them the frames. The first-named craftsman purchased the rough plates from the glass house, and carried out all the processes of grinding, polishing and silvering.

The joiner made the frame, together with the mouldings, if any, and it was then handed to the carver to execute the ornament. The craftsman who carved looking-glass frames was a specialist in carving articles which were afterwards gilded, and he therefore worked in conjunction with the gilder, the partnership being described as "carvers and gilders."

Fig. 38. A SMALL LOOKING-GLASS
in narrow gilt frame. *Temp.* Queen Anne
(*Collection of J. S. Sykes, Esq.*)

Carvers and gilders from the seventeenth up to the nineteenth century made also picture frames, the frames of console and side tables and stands of cabinets, all of which were gilt.

John Pelletier, "Carver and Guilder," according to an account dated 1700, supplied for Hampton Court Palace numerous "Marble Tables," for which he charged £28 each for "Carving and Guilding" the frames. Other marble tables were also supplied with the frames "all white," which expression meant that they were un-gilt.

The frame-carver worked chiefly in soft wood, usually deal, and not in hard woods like oak and mahogany. He executed pieces of particular quality in lime wood, a wood which was especially suitable for the carver's chisel.

The following newspaper advertisements are illustrative of the trade of the looking-glass-maker with its combination with the trades of the cabinet-maker and upholsterer.

"*The London Gazette.* June 14. to June 18. 1688.

"All sorts of Cabimet (sic) Work to be sold, as Cabinets, Scretores, Chest of Drawers, Tables, Stands and Looking-Glasses, to be sold a very good Peniworth by Henry Iden, living lately at the Sign of the Looking-Glass in Ludgate street, who designs to dispose of all in 14 Days. He liveth now in Bell yard in Carter Lane."

As the above-mentioned tradesman lived at "the Sign of the Looking-Glass" and advertised both cabinet ware and glasses for sale, he was probably a looking-glass-maker as well as a cabinet-maker. "Tables, Stands and Looking Glasses" were favourite articles of furniture in the late seventeenth century. Such combinations comprised a table, generally used as a dressing table flanked by a pair of stands for candlesticks, and a looking-glass

Fig. 39. DETAIL OF LOOKING-GLASS, illustrated Fig. 38, showing gilt gesso cresting decorated with unusual motif of cupid's head and wings. Note the wide, concave bevel to the glass plate

which was hung on the wall above the table. Only a few complete sets out of the very large numbers originally made have survived. A table or a glass, either separate or together, or one or a pair of stands, is all that is left to-day of a set.

"*The London Gazette.* May 1. to May 5. 1690.

"John Hoole, Upholsterer, is removed from the Rose in Cornhil, to the Rose in Bishopsgate-street near Cornhill; who hath new fashioned Silk and Stuff Beds ready standing, Glasses, Tables, and Chests of Drawers, to be sold at reasonable Prices."

This appears to be an advertisement of an upholsterer by trade who sold furniture and looking-glasses which he did not make himself, but purchased from other craftsmen. The upholsterer was always very much more of a shopkeeper than a maker.

"*The Post Man.* October 27. 1715.

"Whereas a great Fire happened on Saturday the 16th instant, in Hungerford Market, and burnt violently through into the Strand, and has very much damaged the House and Goods of Jacob Arbunot, who keeps a Looking Glass Shop at the Royal Cabinet over against Church Court in the Strand, so that he has received a very great Loss, by reason a great many of his Glasses have been broke, having had not time to move, the Fire being all round him, and a great many lost, as well as many of his Houshold Goods. This is therefore to desire any one that has any of his Glasses or Houshold Goods, to return them, and they shall be well Rewarded for their Trouble."

"*The Daily Courant.* January 14. 1716.

"This is to give Notice, That Philip Arbunot, who has kept the great Looking-Glass Shop at the Corner of Villers-street in the Strand for several Years last past, will sell all his Goods at a very Reasonable Rate, he designing to leave off his Trade: The Goods consisting of all Sorts of Looking-Glasses Glass Pannels and Sconces, Cabinets both English and Japan, Scrutores, Tables, Stands, Writing-Desks, Book-Cases, Card-Tables, Dressing-Suits and Chests of Drawers both of Japan and Wallnet-tree; likewise carv'd and gilded Sconces, and all Sorts of China, Tea, and Tea-Tables, Screens and Fire-Screens, Oyl-Pictures, Strong-Boxes, . . ."

Fig. 40.   GILT PIER GLASS of architectual design, with gilt pier table with a support in
the form of dolphins.   *Temp*. George II

Fig. 41. AN OVAL LOOKING-GLASS with glass border decorated with bevelling ; one of a set of four.   *Temp.* Queen Anne
(*Collection of J. S. Sykes, Esq.*)

It would seem likely that these two advertisers, both of the name of Arbunot, were related. Jacob was unquestionably a maker and retailer of looking-glasses, whereas Philip, judging from the long range of articles advertised, was probably more of a shopkeeper.

The mention of glass panels refers to the custom at this period of fitting looking-glasses into the panels of the wainscot. Carved and gilded sconces were looking-glasses fitted with a metal candle branch or pair of branches. Sometimes sconces at this period had the backs fitted with needlework panels instead of looking-glasses (*vide* page 74). The mention that Jacob Arbunot had lost his household goods shows that his residence, his shop and warehouse were all at the same premises. This was the general custom amongst tradesmen in the period of hand-craftsmanship.

"*The Daily Courant*. July 29. 1724.
"JAMES WELCH.
"Glass-Grinder and Looking-Glass-Maker, at his Warehouse behind the Rose and Crown, a Grocer's, in the Broad-Way, Black-Fryers, London, where you may be furnished Wholesale or Retale with great Variety of Peer, Chimney, or Sconce Glasses, fine Dressing-Glasses, Coach, Chariot, or Chair-Glasses, with Plate Sash-Glasses, &c. N.B. Merchants, Shopkeepers, or Country Chapmen may be furnished with the aforementioned Goods, as also all sorts of small Glasses at the lowest Rates. Old Glasses cleaned or made into new Fashions."

James Welch, from his advertisement, would appear to have been primarily a glass-worker, and therefore made and sold looking-glass-plates without their frames, or "Naked Glasses," as they were sometimes called. Such plates were bought by the frame-maker (*vide* Fig. 42), who, after fitting them with frames, either sold them retail or in turn sold them to the shopkeeper. The eighteenth century saw the rise of the shopkeeper who sold house furniture, but who was not a maker.

Pier, chimney and sconce glasses refer to the three principal types of looking-glasses in the eighteenth century. The pier glass was so called because it was designed to hang on a pier wall, *i.e.*, a wall between two windows. In the principal rooms of late seventeenth and eighteenth century houses there were usually three windows which were divided by two piers. This type of room plan accounts for the fact that many pier glasses originally were made in pairs. A chimney-glass was so called because it occupied the position above the

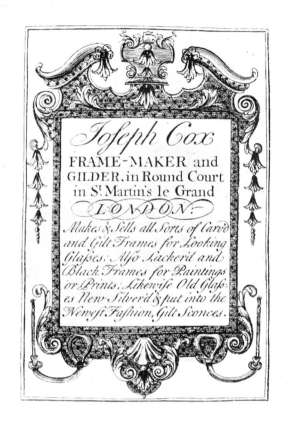

Fig. 42. TRADE CARD of a looking-glass and picture-frame maker. Reproduced from *London Tradesmen's Cards*, by Sir Ambrose Heal

chimney-piece. A sconce, as already mentioned, was a looking-glass with a candle branch.

The frequency of the term sconce, both small and large, in contemporary accounts suggests that all looking-glasses that had candle branches were termed sconces, the name looking-glass being applied to pier and chimney glasses and glasses without branches.

Dressing glasses were designed to stand upon a dressing table. In the first half of the eighteenth century the frames were usually of walnut or japan, being supported on a base fitted with small drawers.

"*The Public Advertiser*. Monday, December 24, 1759.
"Yesterday Morning about Four o'Clock a terrible Fire broke out at Mr. Norman's (late Mr. West's) an eminent Cabinet-maker, Carver and Gilder, in King-street, Covent Garden, which entirely consumed that House, with the Houses of Mr. Bellis, a Jeweller and Toyman on one Side, and Mr. Fortescue, a Linendraper on the other; and greatly damaged two others in Front, viz. Messrs. Bromley and Potts, Stationers; . . ."

The above quoted news item mentions the combination of cabinet-maker and carver and

Fig. 43.   A PIER GLASS of elegant design, one of a pair
Temp. Queen Anne
(Collection of Lord Plender, G.B.E.)

Glasses, Sconces, Chimney-Pieces, Pannel-Glasses very reasonably, or may change your old Looking-Glasses for new ones, or if you have any old Looking-Glasses that want Silvering, shall be done very reasonably. You may also be furnished with Chests of Drawers, or Looking-Glasses at any Price, paying for them Weekly, as we shall agree. Coach Glasses a whole Fore-Glass, Price 4 *l*. Door-Glass, 1 *l*. a Fore-Glass 18*s*.   Pray take care of this Bill." (Bagford 5996, 92.)

The mention of changing old looking-glasses for new ones is indicative of the quickly-changing fashions in looking-glass frames. It was also customary in the eighteenth century to fit new frames of the "Newest Fashion" to old looking-glass plates. This practice was brought about owing to the plate being far more costly than the frame, *vide* Fig. 42. Many looking-glasses are extant which have undergone this treatment, the shape of the glass plate indicating an earlier style of design than the frame.

The advertising of looking-glasses to be sold by " paying for them Weekly, as we shall agree," is evidence that the system of payment by instalments was practised in the early eighteenth century.

The two looking-glasses, Figs. 37 and 44, with veneered walnut frames and carved gilt mouldings are of a type of pier glass which, judging from the large number extant, enjoyed extreme popularity between the years 1720–1750. The laying of the veneer was the work rather of a cabinet-maker than of a joiner-frame-maker who was unskilled in such treatments. This variety of walnut and gilt glass has usually either the motif of an eagle or an escutcheon or shield centering the pediment. Many examples are extant with the floral or oak leaf swags missing at the sides. These swags, only being held in position by

gilder, a partnership which in the middle years of the 18th century was a very practical one owing to the popularity of all types of gilt furniture as well as looking-glasses.

The following is an advertisement of Christopher Thornton, which is in the form of a handbill.   It is undated, but it was probably printed about 1707.

" At *Christopher Thorntons*, living in *Peterstreet* in the *Mint* in *Southwark*, at the *Looking-Glass* near the *Square*, are now to be Sold all sorts of Looking-

glue and pins, often became loose, and in a later age, when the value of the looking-glass became negligible, they were not refixed. In examples of the best quality the veneer is of a figured or burr walnut (*vide* Fig. 37) and not of a plain straight grained walnut chosen for its cheapness. A number of looking-glasses of this type are extant with mahogany veneer instead of walnut. This design of looking-glass was made also with the frame sanded and gilt as an alternative treatment to the walnut veneer (*vide* Fig. 40). The but slight variation in the design of many hundreds of walnut and gilt and entirely gilt looking-glasses of this architectural type shows how strong was the influence of the ruling style at this period.

The pier glass, Fig. 43, with its slender moulded frame decorated with scrolls and eagles' heads and with the hood and apron with ornament cut in gesso, belongs to the period dating from the reign of William III to that of George I, when the frames of looking-glasses obtained the greatest elegance in design. The eagle's head motif was in particular favour during the time of Queen Anne and George I, not only for decorating the frames of glasses but also for chair arms and legs. The looking-glasses, Figs. 45 and 48, also have the same eagle motif incorporated in the design of their cresting.

The looking-glass, Fig. 38, is of unusual design probably because it was made originally for the Spanish market. Looking-glasses for export were designed so as to be in accord with foreign taste.

Philip Arbunot, whose advertisement has already been cited on page 62, made two sconces of an especially elaborate design, which were given by Queen Anne to the Emperor of Morocco.

Phillip Arbunot Cabinetmaker.

For a present from Her Matie to the Emperor of Morocco. For Two large Sconces wth double

Fig. 44.   A PIER GLASS with walnut and gilt frame of architectural character.
Temp. George II
(*Collection of J. S. Sykes, Esq.*)

Branches, finely gilded, being Three foot deep, scoloped, dimond cutt and engraved embollished wth crimson and gold Mosaic work wth flowers, on the bodys of the Glass's &c.   £12 : 7 : 0

These sconces with their "crimson and gold Mosaic work," suggest a gaudiness of design to attract the Emperor's eye. Diamond cut was the term used in the eighteenth century to describe the bevelling of the glass plate.

The oval looking-glass, Fig. 41, with its diamond cut glass border is one of a set of four.

Fig. 45. DETAIL OF PIER GLASS illustrated in Fig. 47 showing carved and gilt cresting with gesso ground

It would seem likely that this set of glasses or sconces was designed originally to hang between the windows of a long room or gallery. Each glass was once fitted with a metal candle branch which is now missing. This set of four oval looking-glasses came from Clumber, Nottinghamshire, a seat of the Duke of Newcastle, for whose eighteenth-century ancestor they were undoubtedly made.

In the reign of William III, Gerreit Jensen, the king's cabinet-maker,[1] supplied numerous oval sconces both large and small for Kensington and other palaces. The following item for a set of sconces, which appears in one of Jensen's bills recorded in the Royal Wardrobe Accounts for 1696, might apply equally to the Clumber examples :

"For 8 Large glasse Ovall Sconces with two branches the frames glasse . . £80."

Looking-glasses framed by a wide diamond cut glass border contained by a narrow wooden bead or moulding similar to the oval glass illustrated, were particularly in fashion during the reigns of William III and Queen Anne. The bevelling to the borders of such glass-framed mirrors was often of an elaborate character, and was sometimes further ornamented with engraving.

The following advertisement shows that bevelling or diamond work was sometimes carried out mechanically and not by hand.

The Engine for Grinding, Pollishing, and Cutting Looking-Glass Plates (for which a Patent is granted by His Majesty) by which Glass is truly Ground and Pollished with the best black Pollish: And also the Borders cut most curiously hollow, and with a better Lustre than any hertofore done. The Warehouse is kept at Mr. Richard Robinson's, at the Flower-Pot in Beaufort-street in the Strand, where Attendance is given every day, from 8 till 12 at Noon, where all sorts of the said Looking-Glass and Coach-Glass Plates are to be had at a reasonable Rate. There also are sold the new-invented Frames for Coach-Glass Plates, or for Windows, of 3 quarters of an inch broad, made of Metal of a Gold colour. (Cf. The London Gazette, Nov. 14–17, 1698.)

[1] Cf. Gerreit Jensen. R. W. Symonds. Connoisseur, Vol. XCV.

Fig. 47. A TALL PIER GLASS with two plates contained in scarlet japan frame, surmounted by carved and gilt cresting. *Temp.* George I

Fig. 46. A PIER GLASS with bevelled glass borders contained in narrow gilt mouldings ; the crest of its original owner being inset in shield. *Temp.* Queen Anne

71

The Engine Looking-glass Warehouse, as it was afterwards called, apparently left off its trade in 1710, as an advertisement appeared in *The Tatler* of April 29th of that year advertising the auction sale of looking-glasses and stating that " no more of the Engine-Work to be had after this sale."

An alternative method to diamond cutting and engraving for ornamenting the glass frames of looking-glasses was to paint a design on the back side of the glass. This treatment, which was much in favour during the reigns of William III and Queen Anne, is called *verre eglomisé*. It was a method that was copied from the French, the designs employed being often arabesque patterns strongly French in character. The " crimson and gold Mosaic work with flowers " of the Emperor's sconces was probably this type of decoration. The following is a newspaper advertisement describing a glass with a *verre eglomisé* frame.

The Daily Courant.
August 24, 1727.
Stolen out of the Shop of Benjamin
Goddison, Cabinet-Maker, at the Golden Spread-Eagle in Long-Acre, on or about the 5th Day of this present August, a large old-fashioned Glass Sconce, in a Glass Frame, with Gold Flowers painted on the Glass Frame, and a green Ground, the Bottom Border of the Frame is Wanting : This is to give Notice, that if any Person shall bring the said Glass, or give any Account of it to the said Benjamin Goddison, shall receive three Guineas Reward.

The mention of a " green Ground " in the description is because in this process the pattern was usually carried out in gold and the background painted black, red, blue or green. The first named was the most popular, judging from extant glasses.

A PIER TABLE of gilt gesso, the legs decorated with Indian masks. *Temp.* George I.

This table is said to have been saved from the fire which occurred at Nottingham Castle in 1831

(Collection of Lord Plender, G.B.E.)

The above advertisement is evidence that the looking-glass with frame decorated with *verre eglomisé* was considered " old-fashioned " in the year 1727. It is by information of this kind that it is possible to determine the approximate date of a particular type of design.

An early reference to a looking-glass decorated with a painted design is contained in an advertisement of the year 1660. This example being " set " in an ebony frame was probably of continental manufacture. It would seem unlikely, however, that the English looking-glass maker would have allowed much time to pass before he copied such imported examples.

Mercurius Publicus.
Aug. 30–Sept. 6. No. 36.
1660.
Stolen the second of September out of a Dining room in Holborn, a large looking glass set in a Ebony frame a Landskip being drawn at the bottom of the glass with a Shepperdess a lamb a Goat and several other figures, there being a flaw at the top of the glass.

The pier-glass, Fig. 48, with its bevelled-glass frame and shaped head, shows the skill that the looking-glass-maker in the time of Queen Anne possessed in designing ornament. The unusual carved and gilt cresting with its varied motifs—a shell, a pair of eagles's heads and scrolled strap-work—is a particularly happy invention ; it amply fulfils its object by giving the frame the necessary amount of enrichment without obscuring or weakening the structural form. This looking-glass has no candle branches and therefore it cannot be termed a sconce, being unquestionably designed as a pier-glass to hang between the windows of a room.

Pier-tables and pier-glasses were made *en suite.* The survival of pier-tables decorated with gilt gesso (sometimes they are in pairs) is an indication that, originally, each had its attendant looking-glass, also with a gesso frame to match.

It would seem likely that the pier-glass in a walnut and gilt frame, similar to the two examples illustrated, was also supplied when required with a pier-table, which, to match the glass, was of veneered walnut probably with the carving and mouldings enriched with gilding. The pier-table matched in material and treatment—whether of gilt gesso, veneered walnut, japan or carved wood and gilt—its attendant glass, rather than in the use of similar ornamental motifs.

Pier-tables have suffered a higher rate of destruction than pier-glasses (especially is this so as regards the gesso pier-table) ; a glass hangs on a wall where it is out of the way, and unlike a table it is not constantly being moved about, therefore it is less likely to come to harm. On the other hand, a table, particularly the top, when of gesso, veneered walnut or japan, is far more susceptible to damage.

Pier- and chimney-glasses and sconces, as the 18th century advanced, came under the influence of the various succeeding styles of design— the architectural style with its accompanying pediments, entablatures and pilasters gave way to French rococo, which in turn was succeeded by the extravagancies of the Gothic and Chinese tastes. The second half of the century saw the return to a more restrained and simpler design composed of " light and elegant ornaments " borrowed from classic architecture ; this style was influenced to a great degree by the work of Robert Adam.

The design of the English looking-glass was at its best during the reigns of William III, Queen Anne and George I. During this period the size of the looking-glass plate was considered an all-important feature. The houses and mansions of the

Fig. 48. A PIER GLASS (one of a pair) with bevelled glass frame and carved wood cresting, gilt. *Temp*. Queen Anne
(*Courtesy of H. M. Lee & Sons*)

73

quality and the nobility were planned with lofty rooms and in consequence the demand was for glasses of tall dimensions. Looking-glass-makers competed with each other in the production of tall pier-glasses and the larger the size of the plate the more expensive was the looking-glass.

"Large Looking-glass Plates, the like never made in England before, both for size and goodness, are now made at the old Glass house at Foxhall, known by the name of the Duke of Buckinghams House, Where all persons may be furnished with rough plates from the smallest sizes to those of six foot in length, and proportionable breadth, at reasonable rates."

(Cf. *The Post Man*, February 13th–15th, 1700.)

In contemporary sale catalogues the large size of the looking-glasses was commented upon in order to attract buyers.

"To be Sold by Auction . . . at a Great House the Lower End of Spring Garden, near Admiralty Office.

"The Entire Furniture of a Person of Quality . . . consisting of Damask, Mohair, and other Standing Beds and Bedding, fine Tapestry Hangings, Persia, Smyrna, and Turkey Carpets, fine Japan Cabinets, Chests, Screens, and other Curiosities . . . likewise large Pier and Chimney Glasses, fine Carved and Gilt Sconces. . . .

"N.B. There are two of the finest large Pier-Glasses in London, whole Plates, one 7 Foot by 3 Foot 6 Inches, the other 5 Foot 9 Inches by 3 Foot 6 Inches, to be sold in the said Sale."

(Cf. *The Daily Journal*, April 11th, 1728.)

During the reign of George II the design of the looking-glass deteriorated, partly owing to the popularity that it now possessed, which caused its manufacture to be in the hands of many small makers, both London and provincial, who were unskilled as ornamentalists, and also to the change in style from the architectural to the rococo, which took place in the middle years of the 18th century.

It is seldom that an 18th century newspaper records the fate of a looking-glass; the following account therefore of a fire, an Irishman and a looking-glass appears worthy of quotation.

"Yesterday Morning at 2 o'clock a Fire broke out in Mr. Hyde's Livery Stable in Old Bond-street, which burnt great Part of the said Stable. . . .

"An honest Irishman, who lived in the Yard where the Fire began, willing to save a Looking-Glass, for which his Wife had a great Value, threw it out of the Window into the Street, and broke it all to Pieces."

(Cf. *The London Daily Post and General Advertiser*, January 22nd, 1740.)

A SCONCE in gilt gesso frame with needlework panel inset. *Temp.* Queen Anne. (*Collection of Geoffrey Hart, Esq.*)

CHAPTER V

ENGLISH JAPAN AND ORIENTAL LACQUER FURNITURE

Fig. 49. INTERIOR VIEW OF CABINET SHOWN IN PLATE V. The painted floral designs, with Japan tortoise-shell borders on the doors, are an unusual treatment

IN the late seventeenth century England was flooded with every variety of imported goods from the East Indies, China and Japan.

" As ill Weeds grow apace, so these Manufactured Goods from *India* met with such a kind reception, that from the greatest Gallants to the meanest Cook-Maids, nothing was thought so fit, to adorn their persons, as the Fabricks of *India*; nor for the ornament of Chambers like *India-Skreens, Cabinets, Beds* and *Hangings*; nor for Closets, like *China* and *Lacquered Ware*; . . ." (Cf. *A Discourse of Trade, Coyn, and Paper Credits*, 1697.)

So great was the craze for " Indian goods " in the late seventeenth and early eighteenth centuries that shops known as " Indian shops " sprang into existence for the display and sale of imported Oriental wares.

Through India shops to Motteux's or the Change,
Where the tall jar erects its stately pride
With antic shapes in China's azure dy'd ;
There careless lies a rich brocade unroll'd,
Here shines a cabinet with burnish'd gold.
(Cf., Dodsley, *The Toy Shop*, 1735.)

The following is an advertisement of the sale of the shop goods of Mrs. Mary Hunt, " *Indian* woman." This advertisement is of particular interest, as it reveals the type and variety of wares in an Indian shop :

" Fine Indian Cabinets, Indian Tea-Tables and Boxes, and Indian Bowls ; a fine Indian Chintze Bed, Indian Quilts and Counterpains, &c. A large Parcel of China, a large Parcel of Indian Fans, &c. Strip'd and plain Muslins, and fine Cambricks, Sheets and Table-Linen, &c. Plate and Rings, Chocolate and Tea, and Indian Pictures. . . ." (Cf. Brit. Mus. Bagford : 5996.)

75

The Indian shops were supplied from the auction sales held by the East India Company. Several small trading companies formed in the late seventeenth and early eighteenth centuries also auctioned Indian goods. The two following advertisements are notices of such sales :

" The Japan Company will sell all sorts of Lacquer'd Japan and China Ware, at Garraway's Coffee-house in Exchange-Alley. . . ." (Cf. *The Daily Courant*, November 12th, 1709.)

" To be Sold by the Charon Company at the Marine Coffee-house in Birchin-Lane . . . Lacker'd Tea-Tables, Cabinets, Writing-Desks, China-Ware, and various sorts of Goods. . . . (Cf. *Ibid*, October 11th, 1708.)

Indian shops were not the only dealers in imported lacquer furniture, as many cabinet-makers and upholsterers sold Indian cabinets, screens and tea-tables.

The merchants importing lacquered wares, in order to promote their trade, sent out to the East " Patterns and Models of all sorts of Cabinet Goods " to be copied by the Chinese craftsmen. This was the inevitable result of the development of the trade, as oriental lacquer furniture that was used by the Chinese, apart from cabinets, did not harmonise with English methods of furnishing. It would seem that there were different varieties and qualities of lacquer ware according to the province or country from which it came. The lacquer made in Japan was recognised by all contemporary writers as the best, and superior to the wares of China and the province of Tonquin.

" The finest comes from *Jappan*, at so dear a Rate, that it will not turn to Account any more than the coursest, which our Artists can out-do ; Therefore the best *China* is advisable." (Cf. *An Account of the Trade in India:* Charles Lockyer, 1711.)

The term " right Japan," often found in contemporary inventories and advertisements, would appear to mean that the article was of the genuine oriental lacquer and not the English imitation. The expression " Japan " in the late 17th and 18th centuries was applied not only to lacquer furniture but to china and silver ware and consequently this term would seem to refer to the oriental design composed of birds, flowers, figures and temples with which the article was decorated. Oriental lacquer furniture being invariably decorated with such designs was termed accordingly " Japan " and English lacquer furniture was also called " Japan " for the same reason. This term was also applied to the process and to the workman—japanning and japanner. The term " India " or " Indian " denoted that an article came from the East.

The popularity of this " Indian " lacquer furniture in the time of Charles II brought into being the trade of the English japanner. Japanning was the European method of

Fig. 50. DETAIL of Japan work of Cabinet illustrated in Colour Plate VI

imitating oriental lacquer. It was as a contemporary writer defines, "the art of covering bodies by grounds of opaque colours in varnish; which may either be afterwards decorated by painting or gilding, or left in a plain state."[1] The oriental lacquer made from the resin of gum trees was in every way superior in quality and technique to the English japan made of paint and varnish. The latter, however, made up for its defects by its greater decorative value, i.e., it was made in a wider range of different coloured grounds. Oriental lacquer was chiefly confined to a black or dark brown ground; English japan was made with grounds not only of black and white but of all colours.[2]

The existence in the one market of these two varieties of lacquer furniture—the imported "Indian" and the home produced "Japan" —soon caused a rivalry between the merchant and the japanner. The japanner petitioned Parliament to suppress the importation of the oriental product, which, he declared, "will not only tend to the Ruine of the Japan-Trade here in *England*, but also obstruct the Transportation of our *English lacquer* to all *Europe*."[3] The result of this dispute was a victory for the English japanner. Import duties were placed upon East Indian goods, and the trade in oriental lacquer furniture consequently decreased in volume.

Japanning was in fashion from the reign of Charles II to the first part of that of George II. The late 17th century and the first quarter of the 18th century was the period when the best work was executed.

> "The *Japan* is brought to that perfection that it not only outdoes all that is made in *India*, but vies for its

lacquer with the Japan Lacquer itself; and there is hopes of imitating its best Draught and Figures." (Cf., *A Collection of Improvement of Husbandry and Trade*, July 20th, 1694. John Houghton.)

In 1695 japanned furniture was so popular that a company called "The Patentees for Lacquering after the Manner of Japan" was formed for its production and sale. In *The Flying Post*, November 23rd–26th, 1695, this company advertised a sale by lottery of "several Parcels of fine Japan'd Goods . . . Cabinets, Scretores, Tables, Stands, Looking-glasses, Tea Tables, Chimney-pieces, &c., being all fresh and new made . . ."

Like all other innovations of the same period, japanning was practised by amateurs and taught in schools. Numerous books were written on the subject giving full instructions for practising the craft.[4]

[4] The earliest and most comprehensive was *A Treatise of Japanning and Varnishing*, 1688, by John Stalker and George Parker. A work of great variety and extreme interest.

[1] *The Handmaid to the Arts*, 2nd Edition. 1764.
[2] In a work entitled *Polygraphice*, by William Salmon, 8th Edition, 1701, the author mentions the following colours and treatments for Japan work: "Black, White, Blew, Red (Common, deep and pale), Olive, Chestnut, Lapis Lazuli, Marble and Tortoise Shell."
[3] Cf., *Furniture from the Indies*. Parts I, II & III. Arts. R. W. Symonds. *Connoisseur*, Vols. XCIII & XCIV, where this aspect of the subject has been dealt with at greater length.

Fig. 51. DETAIL of Japan work of Cabinet illustrated in Colour Plate V

77

Fig. 52. INTERIOR VIEW OF CABINET illustrated in Colour Plate VI

The japanner was a separate craftsman ; the trade to which he was most closely allied being that of the gilder. He was, however, dependent upon the cabinet-maker and the chair-maker who supplied him with the furniture upon which he exercised his craft. It is not possible to say to what extent a master-japanner worked on his own account. In some cases he bought the carcasses of his furniture from the cabinet-maker and after treatment with japan sold the finished article. This was probably the method of James Bradford :

" At the Sign of the Angel, the Corner of Poppin's-Alley in Fleetstreet ; will be Sold by Auction, the Goods of James Bradford, Japanner, he going to leave off Shop-Keeping : consisting of Cabinets, Desks, and Book-Cases, Chests of Drawers, Union Suits, Tables, Peer-Glasses, Sconces, Screen-Frames, Glasses, Dressing-Glasses, with all sorts of Japaned Goods, . . . " (Cf., *The Weekly Journal*, March 26, 1714.)

The following also appears to be the advertisement of a craftsman who confined his trade mostly to the production and sale of japanned furniture, or possibly the advertiser was a shopkeeper only and not a maker.

" . . . a Parcel of fine Goods, . . . the stock of Richard Jones ; at the Sign of the Japan Cabinet near King Edward's Stairs in Wapping, he leaving off his Trade :

The Goods consisting of very fine Japan Cabinets, Desks, and Book-Cases, Chests of Drawers, Japan and Wallnut, likewise plain Wainscoat, and fine Japan Trunks, Beaufets, Corner Cupboards, Looking-Glasses and Sconces, &c." (Cf., *The Daily Courant*, December 7th, 1720.)

A cabinet-maker in a small way of business would send probably his furniture that he wanted japanned to a japanner, whereas one with a large establishment would have his own journeymen japanners working for him. Many cabinet-makers stocked " India Japan'd " furniture which they had bought at the auction sales and sold it side by side with the English japan of their own making. The following advertisement would appear to belong to a cabinet-maker who carried on his business in this way.

" At the Cabinet on Ludgate-hill still remains to be sold, at very low rates, the following goods of Mr. Pistor lately deceas'd, being all to be disposed of by Lady-day next. Three fine Japan'd and 1 walnut Cabinetts, 1 fine walnut and 1 India Scrutore, 1 Wainscott Desk and Book-case on Drawers, 1 Japan'd Tortoiseshel and 1 black Plate Case, and 3 fine Prince-wood strong Boxes, 1 fine inlaid Copper-fram'd large Glass, Table and Stands ; right India Japan'd large Glass, Table and Stands ; 1 White Japan'd Glass and Table . . . 1 Japan'd Chimney Glass, some Japan'd swing Glasses . . . several Walnut Black and Japan'd

PLATE V

A CABINET AND STAND
of yellow japan.   Early 18th century
(*Collection of Geoffrey Hart, Esq.*)

Onamber Tables, &c. (Cf., *The Spectator*, March 22nd, 1711.)

Firms of cabinet-makers, who carried on an export trade with Spain and Portugal, probably had their own workshops for japanning, owing to the greater part of the furniture exported to these two countries being of japan. The couch and chair of scarlet japan, illustrated Figs. 56 and 57, were made originally by Giles Grendey of Clerkenwell (the chair bears Grendey's label on the seat-rail) for export to Spain. The suite to which this chair and couch belong was found in Spain several years ago.

When the English cabinet- and chairmakers were making furniture for export they amended its design and treatment so that it would be more in accord with foreign tastes. Japan furniture of bright scarlet and gold must have been especially favoured for this foreign trade, judging from the quantity of English scarlet japanned chairs, cabinets, bureau bookcases and clockcases that have been found on the continent within recent years. Much of this English japanned furniture that is in Spain has the scarlet of a faded tint owing to exposure to the sun.

The following excerpt from the *Parent's and Guardian's Directory*, 1761, give some interesting details of the japanner's trade.

"Japanning is a very curious art; and those ingenious boys are only fit for it, who have a natural taste for drawing and painting. The youth, therefore, who is put apprentice to this business, ought to learn to draw to great perfection. The Japanner embellishes with painting and japanning all sorts of fine cabinets, chests of drawers, corner-cupboards, &c, all made of wood; besides tea-boards, waiters, and other utensils, made of copper, &c. The japanning part is done over the painting, by washing the piece all over with a fine varnish, and drying it before a good fire. The masters take 20 or 30 L with an apprentice: who, if a good hand at painting, will be able to get between 20 and 30 s. a week, and perhaps more: and, with 50 or 60 L. may be enabled to set up master."

The date of this description shows that in the third quarter of the 18th century, the japanner was still carrying on his trade. By this time, however, the decline had set in, for in 1758 it was written that "This [japanning] is not at present practised so frequently on chairs, tables and other furniture of houses,

Fig. 53. AN EXAMPLE OF EMBOSSED JAPAN WORK with scarlet background, taken from a door panel of a Queen Anne Bureau Bookcase

except tea-waiters, as formerly."[1]

With the decline of the craft the design lost its character and the technique no longer possessed the quality that was so outstanding a feature of the japan work of the period of William III and Queen Anne. Finally, about 1780, an inferior method of treating chairs and tables with painted decoration came into vogue, and although it was termed japanning, it possessed none of the quality of the earlier and original work.

The technical quality of japanning varied to a considerable degree. An essential feature that is emphasized by all contemporary writers on the art is that the surface should be perfectly smooth and highly polished, outstanding characteristics of the surface of all oriental

---

[1] *The Handmaid to the Arts*, 1st Edition, 1758.

Fig. 54. DETAIL showing the interior containing small drawers of the incised lacquer cabinet, illustrated Fig. 55

lacquer.[1] Elaborate and detailed instructions are given to achieve this result. These instructions apply not only to the preparation of the wood before the application of the japan, but also to the final polishing of the surface after the japan work has been carried out. In the former process one authority recommends that " for the tops of Tables, Boxes, sides of Cabinets, &c. where the Wood is ordinary and rough Grain'd, as Deal, Oak, &c. you may take common or Joyners Glew, dissolve it in Water till it is fine and thin, into which put the finest Saw-dust, till it is indifferently thick. Then with a Brush fit for that purpose lay it all over your Work; and being dry, repeat it so often till all the Roughness and Grain of the Wood is sufficiently hidden. After two or three days let a Cabinet-maker scrape it with his Scraper as Pear-tree and Olive-wood are done, to make it as smooth and even as may be; then Varnish it as formerly directed."[2]

Nearly all japan furniture had the carcass of deal, and in the case of chairs, beech was generally employed. Deal being a soft wood, was a bad foundation, as after it had become matured the grain showed through the japanning. In japanned furniture of good quality, especially in the case of cabinets, the carcass was first veneered with a close-grained and smooth wood, " of all which Pear-tree is the first in Estimation." The surface formed by a close-grained veneer made an excellent foundation for the japan.

The polishing of the japan received as much care as the preparation of the wood. The degree of quality in the polishing signifies the original quality of the piece. Pieces of the best quality had the japan highly polished, whereas in inferior work the surface was left varnished only.

" Having varnished your piece sufficiently over and being perfectly dry, according to the Nature and Curiosity of it, it is to go either unpolished or to be polished."[2]

The following is from a contemporary account of the polishing of black japan:

" But in Polishing, you must work at it till it is almost smooth, and so let it lye for two days; then Polish it again almost enough, and again let it lye six days: and, lastly, Polish it fully, and so clear it

[1] " Lacquer'd-ware [Oriental] should be without Specks, smooth, and of so shining a Black, that you may see your Face in it . . ." Cf., *An Account of the Trade in India*, by Charles Lockyer, 1711.

[2] *Polygraphice:* 8th Edition. By William Salmon, 1701.

Fig. 55. A CHINESE CABINET of decorated incised lacquer mounted on original English ebonised elmwood stand. *Temp.* Charles II
(*Collection of J. S. Sykes, Esq.*)

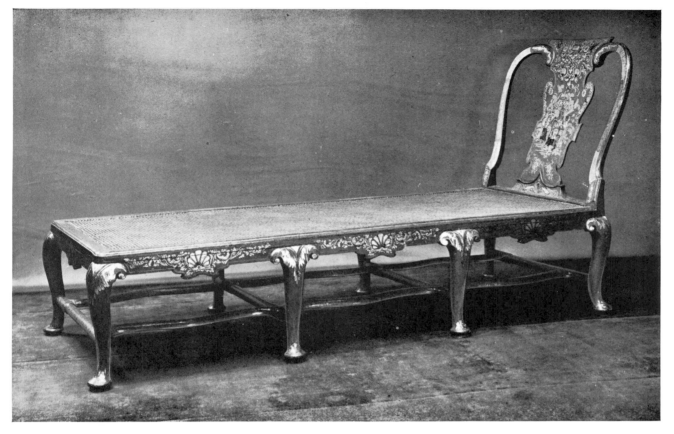

Fig. 56. A COUCH in scarlet and gold japan work with cane seat. This couch and the chair illustrated in Fig. 57 belonged to a suite of furniture made by Giles Grendey for export to Spain. *Temp.* George I

up with Oil and Lamp-black as formerly directed; so will you have a good black Japan, scarcely at all inferior to the true *Indian.*"[1]

The evidence from these contemporary quotations shows to what degree English japan furniture differed in quality. This variation in quality is reflected in the japan furniture that is extant. The best quality work has a surface perfectly smooth with a high polish. Pieces of poor quality, possess a rough surface, varnished but not polished.

In considering the three cabinets which are illustrated, the cabinet, Figs. 54 & 55, is a Chinese example which was imported into England in the late 17th century. Apart from its fine preservation, it is unusual in the respect that it is of incised lacquer instead of the more ordinary raised or "embossed" lacquer. Another of its unusual features is that it has a brown coromandel ground instead of a black ground. The partitioning holding the drawers of the interior is marked with Chinese characters; the drawer linings are of a soft

wood which is stained black; the rough dove-tailing and general coarse construction of the drawers are of typical oriental workmanship, the bottoms being fixed by pins.

The incised variety of oriental lacquer was a far more favoured treatment for screens than cabinets, judging from the number of each that is extant. Many cabinets decorated with incised lacquer were made by the English cabinet-maker from imported lacquer screens or boards. Such cabinets, however, differ from the example illustrated by the fact that when the screen panels were cut it was not possible to preserve the completeness of the design, in consequence of which neither on the doors nor on the sides is the pattern complete.

The following are items taken from a contemporary bill of a japanner, Thos. Rymell, who carried out work for Queen Mary II. These items appear to be for cutting up panels of oriental lacquer ware for re-use in the decoration of cabinets, tables and other articles.

---

[1] *Polygraphice*, 8th Edition. By William Salmon, 1701.

Fig. 57. ARMCHAIR in scarlet and gold lacquer, made by Giles Grendey. *Temp.* George I

Her Maj^tie Bill.
Thos Rymell Japanner
1694
agust y^e 5
For Cuting y^e Pannels out
of foure screns .. .. 2 : 0 : 0
For Cuting a large Japan
chest & sliting .. .. 1 : 5 : 0
For 2 birds of rite Japan &
leting them into 2 tea tables 0 : 12 : 0

This practice is condemned by Stalker and Parker.

" I think no person is fond of it, or gives it house-room, except some who have made new Cabinets out of old Skreens. And from that large old piece, by the help of a Joyner, make little ones, such as Stands or Tables, but never consider the situation of their figures ; so that in these things so torned and hacked to joint a new fancie, you may observe the finest hodgpodg, and medly of Men and Trees turned topsie turvie. . . ."

(Cf., *A Treatise on Japanning and Varnishing*, 1688.)

Rooms were also wainscoted with " India Japan," which probably took the form of panelling constructed of oriental incised lacquer boards.

To be SOLD by AUCTION . . . all the Goods in the House of the Hon. the lady Monson, lately deceas'd, in Pall-Mall, consisting of great variety of rich Furniture, Pictures, Plate and China ; particularly two Rooms Wainscotted with curious old India Japan, fix'd with wooden Screws, for the conveniency of moving. (Cf., *The Daily Post*, July 5, 1725.)

The English japanner also imitated this incised oriental lacquer, and in a contemporary work entitled *Polygraphice* (8th Edit., 1701) the author, William Salmon, gives a detailed account of how " Bantam Work " (the term applied to incised lacquer) should be carried out. The name Bantam suggests that this particular variety of lacquer had some connection with the province of Bantam in the Island of Java. Up to 1682 Bantam, besides being the headquarters of the English pepper trade, was also a clearing station for English and Chinese products. After this date the Dutch took possession and Bantam became a Dutch trading centre. Presumably, the term " Bantam " as applied to incised lacquer ware originated when Bantam was under the English during the reign of Charles II.

Another name than Bantam work for this incised lacquer was " cut-work." James Moore, a cabinet-maker to Frederick, Prince of Wales, in 1732, charged for cleaning and mending an " India Cut-work Cabbinet." He also charged the sum of £22 for " A new Cutwork Cabbinet made to match ye other."

Fig. 58. TRADE LABEL OF GILES GRENDEY fixed to the underside of seat rail of chair Fig. 57

Fig. 59. A CHAIR made of beech wood decorated with green japan and the carving enriched with gilding and the green japan
ground embellished with floral motifs. *Temp.* Late 17th century
(*In the Collections of the Victoria and Albert Museum*)

87

PLATE VI

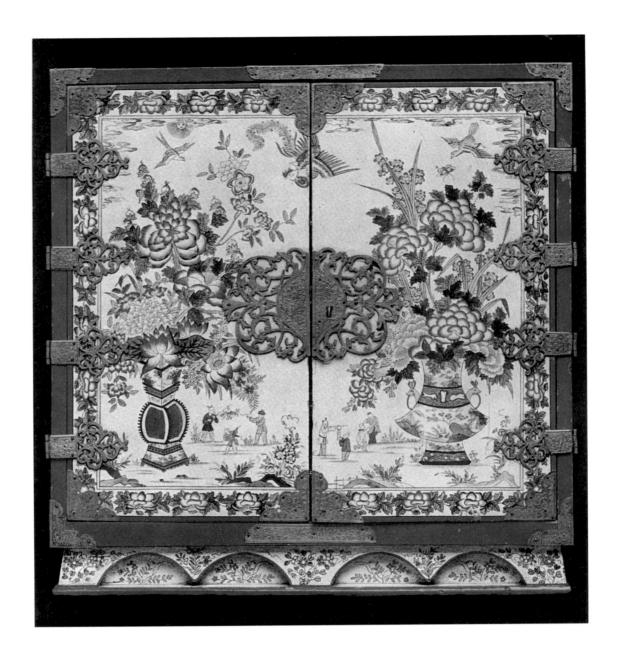

A CABINET OF WHITE JAPAN

of highest quality execution. *Temp.* Queen Anne

(*Collection of Geoffrey Hart, Esq.*)

PLATE VII

A QUEEN ANNE CABINET OF SCARLET JAPAN
supported on carved and silvered Charles II Stand
(*Collection of J. S. Sykes, Esq.*)

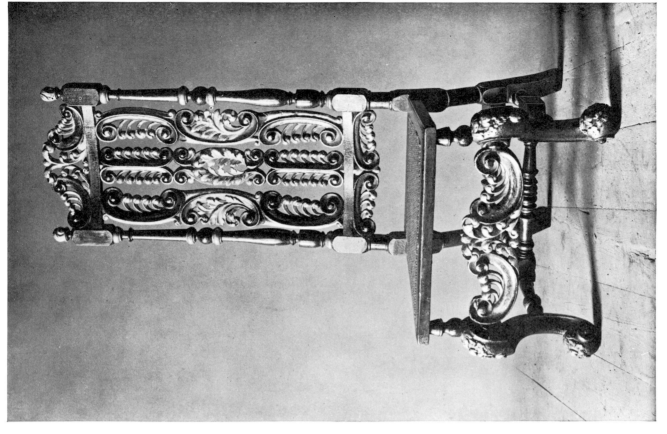

Fig. 61. A BEECH WOOD CHAIR originally decorated in scarlet japan, the carving enriched with silver foil. *Temp.* Late 17th century
(*In the Art Industrial Museum, Copenhagen*)

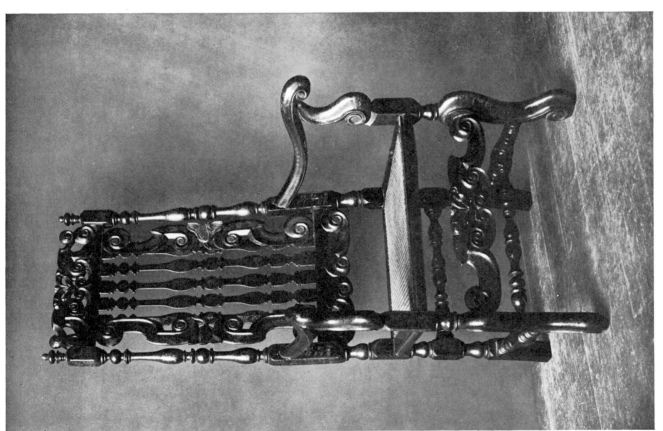

Fig. 60. A BEECH WOOD ARMCHAIR decorated with black japan with gilt floral embellishment. *Temp.* Late 17th century

The "*India* japan" cabinet on its arrival in England was mounted on a stand, usually carved and gilt, the product of the carver and gilder. In the late seventeenth century these cabinet stands were generally designed with four legs connected on the front and sides by deep apron pieces, carved with motifs of amorini amidst acanthus foliage. Such stands were usually treated with silver leaf which, when lacquered or varnished, took on a golden tint. The reason for this expedient was that in the 17th century gold leaf was costly, and, therefore, lacquered silver was employed as a cheaper treatment.

The white japan cabinet, illustrated colour plate VI and Fig. 52, is an example of outstanding quality. The execution of the drawing and the high lustrous polish indicate its exceptional merit.

The yellow ground cabinet, illustrated colour plate V and Fig. 49, is another example of the fine quality that English japanning can sometimes achieve. The free execution of the design indicates that it must have been the work of an artist of considerable talent, very different from the mediocre draughtsmanship, so common a feature of the ordinary type of japan furniture. The floral panels with tortoiseshell japan borders decorating the backs of the doors are a most distinctive feature of the cabinet when open, *vide* Fig. 49. The simple and excellent design of the japanned stand is unusual, as cabinet stands were not generally of such good design; suffering in many cases from an over-lavish use of ornament.

These two cabinets, white and yellow respectively, are to-day of the greatest rarity, for the reason that the percentage of destruction of light ground japan furniture was far higher owing to it being more susceptible to damage than dark ground japan.

The chair and stool, *vide* Figs. 60 & 62, are

Fig. 62. A BEECH WOOD STOOL japanned black with gilt floral embellishment. One of a pair.
Temp. Late 17th century
(*Collection of Lord Plender, G.B.E.*)

examples decorated with black japan. The japanning of chairs in the late 17th century was a very favourite practice of the chair-makers. They made their best and most expensive chairs of walnut, which they polished and their cheaper chairs they made of beech, which they japanned in various colours. In the Royal Wardrobe Accounts many chairs are described as "Japand black"; other treatments mentioned were "Japand purple," "blue and white," "Japan China" and "fine greene Japan."

The design of the 17th century chair did not permit of any large plain areas for decoration; sprigs of flowers and small floral swags and bands were therefore the most usual motifs. It is probable that many of these japanned chairs were not ornamented in this way, but were plain with only the carving and the turning enriched with lacquered silver leaf. Few examples, however, have survived with either the decoration or silvered enrichment intact, as when a chair became shabby and worn the usual custom was for it to receive a coat of paint which obliterated the original treatment. An example of this is the chair, Fig. 61; under several coats of black paint the original colour— a bright scarlet—was discovered and the carving was also found to be silvered.

Judging from inventories, advertisements and sale catalogues, japan furniture, owing to the great popularity it enjoyed, must have been made in larger quantities than any other variety of furniture during the late 17th century and the first forty years of the 18th century. That such a very small percentage of the original output has survived is due to much of it being made of deal and beech—soft woods extremely susceptible to the worm—and to its painted and varnished surface registering every scratch and damage caused by domestic use.

CHAPTER VI

THOMAS TOMPION (1639-1713)

" The great Tompion had never made Watches, had he not first made Hob-nails."[1]

PRIOR to the reign of Charles II the craft of English watch- and clock-making was in its infancy. After the accession of this monarch several notable horological inventions were made, which caused a considerable improvement in the time-keeping of both watches and clocks. The two seventeenth-century English scientists to whom most honour is due for their horological discoveries are Dr. Robert Hooke, F.R.S. (1635-1703), and the Rev. Edward Barlow (1639-1719).

It was, however, Thomas Tompion who, by applying the theories of these two men and by " his excellent skill in making watches and clocks and not less curious and dexterous in constructing and hard working of other nice mechanical instruments,"[2] helped to raise the craft of English watch- and clock-making to the position of second to none in Europe. Tompion in his time was recognized as an horologist and craftsman of the highest order, not only in his own country—where he received the honour of burial in Westminster Abbey— but abroad. In 1732 a German author wrote concerning him as follows :

" Most of these clocks and the best of them were made by Thomas Tompion, as he was considered the best clock-maker in London of his time. In view of this he charged 10 L. sterling for the smallest of his clocks ; similar clocks being obtainable from other clock-makers for 6 or 7 pounds." (*Cf.* Henrich Ludolff Benthem, *Neueröffneter Engeländischer*

Fig. 63. MEZZOTINT PORTRAIT OF THOMAS TOMPION after the painting by Sir Godfrey Kneller

Kirch : und Schulen-Staat, Leipzig, 1732.)

And a work entitled *The Artificial Clock-Maker*, by W. D. [William Derham], 1696, records :

" In the History of the Modern Inventions, I have had (among some others) the assistance chiefly of the ingenious *Dr. H.* [Hooke] and *Mr. T.* [Tompion]. The former being the Author of some, and well acquainted with others, of the Mechanical Inventions of that fertile Reign of King *Charles* II, and the latter actually concerned in all, or most of the late inventions in Clock-work, by means of his famed skill in that, and other Mechanical operations."

Thomas Tompion was the eldest son of Thomas Tompion, a blacksmith, who lived in the village of Northill, Bedfordshire. Tompion the blacksmith had three children : Thomas, the horologist, who was born at Northill and was baptized on July 25th, 1639 ; Margaret, a daughter, born in 1640 ; and James, the youngest, born in 1643.

By 1671, Tompion had already earned repute in his craft, as he was described as a " Great Clockmaker " when he was admitted in this year as a " Brother " to the Clockmakers' Company.[3] In 1691, he was chosen to the Court of Assistants. From 1700 to 1703 he served the offices of Junior, Renter, and Senior Wardens, and became Master in 1703-4.

Both of Tompion's nieces, Elizabeth, the daughter of his brother James, and Margaret, the daughter of his sister Margaret Kent, married clock-makers, George Graham and

---

[1] *The Weekly Journal or British Gazeteer*, January 17, 1719.
[2] Statement made by Hooke concerning Tompion. Quoted by M. Jourdain. Cf. *The City's Jubilee Gift to the King*, " Country Life," November, 1935.

[3] Tompion's admission to the Clockmakers' Company in this manner indicates that he had originally taken his freedom in another company.

Fig. 64. DETAIL SHOWING SIDE OF HOOD AND THE GILDED METAL FRETS OF THE ROYAL CLOCK reproduced in colour plate VIII

buried beside his master in Westminster Abbey.

Edward Banger, who was admitted to the Clockmakers' Company in 1695, was both apprentice and assistant to Tompion, but unlike Graham, who was a scientist and inventor rather than a clock-maker, he designed and made clocks (many of the table type) in collaboration with his uncle; such clocks being identified to-day by the names of both master and pupil—" Tompion & Banger." The quality of the work of these partnership movements are of even greater exactitude and finish than those that were made by Tompion alone.

Tompion left to his nephew Thomas Tompion, the son of his brother James, all the property he owned at Northill and elsewhere in Bedfordshire, together with all sums " which shall be due, or owing from him to me at the time of my death." Tompion junior was also a clock-maker and was apprenticed to Charles Kempe in 1694, and was admitted a member of the Clockmakers' Company in 1702. He appears to have been of little note either as a watch- or clock-maker. There is no extant clock of his make recorded which would imply that if he were working as an assistant to his uncle he retired from the trade of clock-making after Tompion's death when he inherited his property.

The following news item from *The Weekly Packet* of September 24th, 1720, indicates that not many years after Thomas Tompion's death his nephew, presumably after squandering his uncle's estate, stooped to petty theft.

Edward Banger respectively. George Graham, when he was twenty-three, entered Tompion's service, in which he remained until Tompion's death in 1713. Several clocks are extant which are inscribed " Tompion & Graham." Owing to Tompion's never having married, and, therefore, having no direct heir, he left his business and stock-in-trade to his nephew, George Graham.[1]

Graham achieved fame as a scientist and horologist, and was elected a Fellow of the Royal Society; foremost among his inventions were the mercurial pendulum and the " deadbeat escapement." He died in 1751 and was

Fig. 65. DETAIL SHOWING CAST AND CHASED METAL BASE OF CLOCK reproduced in colour plate. (The lower wooden plinth is not original)

---

[1] *The Englishman.* November 28 to December 1, 1713.
GEO. GRAHAM, Nephew of the late Mr. Tho. Tompion, Watch-maker, who lived with him upwards of 17 Years, and managed his Trade for several Years last past; whose Name was joined with Mr. Tompion's for some Time before his Death, and to whom he hath left all his Stock and Work, finished and unfinished; continues to carry on the said Trade, at the late Dwelling-house of the said Mr. Tompion, at the Sign of the Dial and Three Crowns, at the Corner of Water-lane in Fleet-street, London; where all Persons may be accommodated as formerly.

Fig. 66. DETAIL OF HOOD AND DIAL, showing the fine quality of the gilded metal mounts and the figure of Minerva with the cypher of William III on the pedestal below.

(*Collection of J. S. Sykes, Esq.*)

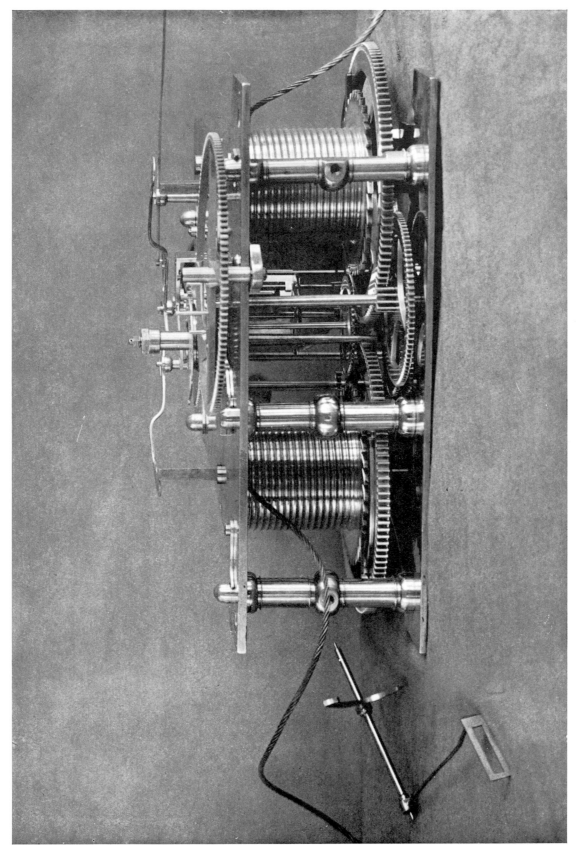

Fig. 67. VIEW THROUGH THE BOTTOM OF THE MOVEMENT OF THE ROYAL CLOCK, showing train of wheels giving three months' duration. The large uppermost wheel in photograph is part of the perpetual calendar work. Note the shutters above winding squares and the interesting hooks which Tompion always used to hold the plates together.

99

" Last Week one Thomas T——n, Nephew of the famous Tompion, the Watchmaker in Fleet-street, was, together with his Wife, committed to Newgate, for picking a Gentlewoman's Pocket (a Wife of a Ship's Mate) of 11 Guineas, upon the River of Thames."

In the *Diary* of Robert Hooke[1] there are numerous references to Thomas Tompion, which not only throw a sidelight on the well-known people of the time that Tompion knew and worked for, but also reveal how much he was indebted to Hooke for disclosing to him his theories and inventions. Undoubtedly this collaboration was of the greatest assistance to Tompion, coming as it did in the early days of his career. Hooke also owed much to so capable a craftsman for the application of his inventions. According to the *Diary* it was in the years 1674–77 that Hooke was in more or less daily communication with Tompion. He generally called upon Tompion, but sometimes the latter visited Hooke, and on rarer occasions dined with him at his house. The *Diary* has also one entry of " Tompion here all night."

There are many references in the *Diary* of Hooke and Tompion with others visiting Garraways, the famous coffee house in Change Alley, Cornhill. Other coffee houses they met at were Joes in Mitre Court, Fleet Street, and Mans in Chancery Lane. On one occasion Hooke mentions "With Godfrey and Tompion at Play." There is

Fig. 68. A YEAR EQUATION CLOCK in Walnut Case with cast and chased gilded mounts. Made by Thomas Tompion about 1700, probably to the order of Sir John Germain and originally at Drayton House, Northamptonshire.
(*Collection of S. E. Prestige, Esq.*)

recorded in the *Diary* many of Hooke's conversations with Tompion about his theories concerning the design and construction of watch and clock movements. The following clearly show how much Tompion was taught by Hooke :

" To Thomkin in Water Lane. Much Discourse with him about Watches. Told him the way of making an engine for finishing wheels, and a way how to make a dividing plate ; about the forme of an arch ; about another way of Teeth work ; about pocket watches. . . ."

" Shewd Tompion in Martins shop how to stay a falling clock weight by a scaffold pole."

" Tompion. I shewd my way of fixing Double Springs to the inside of the Balance wheel. . . ."

" Mr. Tompion here from 10 till 10. He brought clockwork to shew."

" Told him my way of springs by a hammer and anvill, like making pins, which he approved off."

" Tompion here instructed him about the Kings striking clock about bells and about the striking by the help of a spring instead of a pendulum, as also the ground and use of the fly and of the swash teeth."

Several times Hooke records his annoyance with Tompion. " At Tompions scolded with him." And again, " I fell out with him for slownesse," and in another entry " Tompion a Slug." On one occasion it appears as if a quarrel about a watch were likely to terminate their friendship. " At Garaways. Thompion. A clownish churlish Dog. I have limited him to 3 day and will never come neer him more." But within four days Hooke's feelings are appeased as he goes to see " Tompion at 4 p.m." Two days afterwards he

1 *The Diary of Robert Hooke.* (Edited by H. W. Robinson and W. Adams, London). Taylor & Francis. 1935.

is again annoyed and registers his feelings by the following terse entry : " Tompion a Rascall."

A significant entry in the *Diary* reads as follows :

" T o G a r a w a y s, Sir Jonas More[1] and Tompion there, discoursed about spring watch. Tompion said he would ingage &c. but twas but to pump." This suggests that Tompion was not above stealing Hooke's ideas and using them to his own advantage.

In 1675[2] Hooke designed a watch for Charles II. It was made by Tompion, and on Wednesday, April 7th of the same year, Hooke makes the following entry in his diary : " With the King and shewd him my new spring watch, Sir J. More and Tompion there. The King most graciously pleasd with it and commended it far beyond Zulichems. He promised me a patent and commanded me to prosecute the degree. Sir J. More beggd for Tompion."

Later, on August 26th, Hooke again mentions the watch in his *Diary*, when he writes : " I told Mr. Tompion I would not pay him for it but he must expect if (*sic*) from the King."

Fig. 69. DETAIL OF DRAYTON CLOCK (illustrated Fig. 68) showing 80 lb. Weight and Pendulum

Other interesting entries concerning Tompion are that on July 26th, 1675, " Sir Chr Wren bespoke clock of Tompion," and on October 14th of the same year Sir J. Moore " promised to lend Thompion £50," which implies that Tompion at this period had not yet grown prosperous.

The long-case and table clocks illustrated are most worthy examples of the "famed skill" of Thomas Tompion. The long-case clock depicted in the colour plate is so celebrated that only a brief description is necessary. This clock was made by Tompion about 1695–1700 for William III, whose cypher adorns the pedestal which supports the figure of Minerva. It is said to have been made for the bedroom of this monarch at Hampton Court, but owing to the fact that its ticking disturbed the King it was removed. The movement of this remarkable clock goes for three months without rewinding, and it has a perpetual calendar that makes allowance for leap year. Like all Tompion's Royal clocks the cabinet work of the case and the richly gilded mounts are of the finest execution.

The second long case clock, *vide* Fig. 68, was originally at Drayton House, Northamptonshire. It was probably one of the items of furnishing carried out by Sir John Germain (1650–1718). Germain, who was of Dutch descent, accompanied William III to England, and was

---

[1] Sir Jonas Moore (1617–1679). Mathematician and Fellow of the Royal Society.

[2] " The time of these Inventions was about the year 1658, as appears (among other evidence) from this inscription, upon one of the aforesaid double Ballance-Watches, presented to K. *Charles* II, *viz. Robert Hook inven*, 1658. *T. Tompion fecit*, 1675.

" This Watch was wonderfully approved of by the King ; and so the Invention grew into reputation, and was much talked of at home, and abroad. Particularly, its fame flew into *France*, from whence the Dauphine sent for two ; which that eminent Artist Mr. *Tompion* made for him."

(*The Artificial Clock-Maker*. By *W. D*[erham]. 1 Vol. *LONDON*, 1696.)

Fig. 70. SIDE VIEWS OF YEAR MOVEMENT OF DRAYTON CLOCK.   Note the practical method of construction; the heavy weight attached to the barrel is adequately supported on the seat board, the screws of which are visible.   The remaining portion of the train lies between the dial and the front plate.   The pendulum which vibrates behind the dial is visible

Fig. 72. AN ENGRAVING OF DIAL OF EQUATION
CLOCK made by Tompion & Banger in 1703 for George,
Prince of Denmark

Fig. 71. DETAIL OF DIAL OF DRAYTON CLOCK
mercurial gilt and of the highest quality execution

Fig. 73. DETAIL OF HOOD AND DIAL of the Drayton Clock by Thomas Tompion, illustrated Fig. 68
(*Collection of S. E. Prestige, Esq.*)

Fig. 74. A TABLE CLOCK with repeater movement and *grande sonnerie* striking by Thomas Tompion. The case is of veneered ebony with chased and gilt metal mounts ; the finials being designed in the form of tulips. *Temp.* Charles II
(Collection of J. S. Sykes, Esq.)

PLATE VIII

A ROYAL CLOCK

Made by Thomas Tompion for King William III,
for Hampton Court Palace

(*Collection of J. S. Sykes, Esq.*)

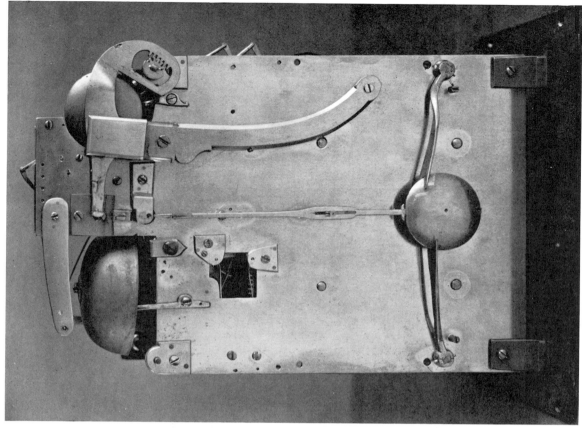

Figs. 75 and 76.   DIAL AND BACK VIEW OF *GRANDE SONNERIE* CLOCK, illustrated Fig. 74, showing the hour and quarter bells and the early rack and pinion device for regulating the length of pendulum.   The forked arms for holding the pendulum which are actuated from the dial are an interesting feature.

created a baronet in 1698. He inherited Drayton through his wife, Lady Mary Mordaunt. It is said that in his alterations to Drayton he endeavoured to make the house resemble as near as possible Hampton Court.[1] This may account for the presence at Drayton of this long case equation clock by Tompion, which is nearly identical in design as regards the movement and the dial with an example made by Thomas Tompion for William III, which is in the possession of H.M. the King. The Royal clock, however, is about five years earlier than the Drayton example, which dates about 1700.

In the Royal Collection is another equation clock,[2] which is of the same type as the one made for William III and the Drayton clock, except that it is by Tompion and his nephew Edward Banger. This equation clock is presumably the identical one which forms the subject of a " Description " in the MS. Department of the British Museum.[3] Evidence in support of this contention is to be found in the similarity of the dial of this Royal clock to a print of the dial of the clock in the " Description." (This print is reproduced, Fig. 72.) Another point of evidence is the fact that the clock in the " Description " was a Royal clock, as it was made for George,

Fig. 77. DETAIL showing the three quarter bells and metal plate upon which movement is fixed of clock illustrated Fig. 74

Prince of Denmark (1653–1708), the consort of Queen Anne. The following is an excerpt from the " Description," which is also applicable to the Drayton clock, with the exception of the perpetual calendar, which was an additional feature fitted to the Royal clock.

" A DESCRIPTION of a very curious Piece of Clockwork, at present in the State Bedchamber in the Royal Palace at Kensington.

" This very curious Piece of Clockwork, was made for his Highness Prince George of Denmark, by Messrs. Tompion & Banger ; & was finished (as I have been informed) in the Year 1703 ; It is inclosed in a very neat Walnutree Case, adorned with brass Mouldings, & other Ornaments.

" This Clock when once wound up, will continue going three hundred & ninety days, before it will require to be wound up a second time ; It shews the hour of the day, & the Minutes, both of the Mean or Equal Time, & of the Apparent or Solar Time ; likewise, the days of the Week, the days of the Month, the months of the Year, the Suns place in the Ecliptick, & what year it is after Bissextile or Leap Year : The Dialplate is twelve inches diameter, having an Elevation in the upper part, as described in Plate the 2d ; which is an exact representation of the Dialplate. [vide Fig. 72.]

" The innermost Circle upon the Plate is for the Hours, it is divided into the hours, & half hours, of the Natural Day, & the hand which points to it makes but one revolution in 24 hours. Next to the Hour Circle, & upon the same Plate, is described the Circle which shews ye minutes of the Equal Time, or the time by the Clock ; the hand which points to it makes but one revolution in two hours, & the Circle is divided into minutes & half minutes contained in that space of time.

" The outermost Circle on the Plate, shews the minutes of the Apparent or Solar time, & is divided in the same manner as the Circle which shews the Equal

[1] English Homes. Late Stuart, by H. Avray Tipping, p. 272.
[2] Both these Royal equation clocks are illustrated and described in Buckingham Palace, by H. Clifford Smith, and Old English Clocks, by F. H. Green.
[3] King's Library. 277.

Fig. 78. A TABLE CLOCK with repeater movement and *grande sonnerie* striking by Thomas Tompion. The case is of veneered ebony with chased and mercurial gilt metal mounts. *Temp.* Charles II. Formerly in the Collection of H.R.H. the Duke of Sussex (1773-1843)

(*Collection of Major Sir John Prestige*)

Fig. 79.   AN ORRERY by THOMAS TOMPION and GEORGE GRAHAM in veneered ebony case with silver dials and mouldings, 9 inches in height.
Circa 1700.   The Orrery, which was an instrument to show the motions of the planets about the sun by means of clockwork, was
invented by George Graham for Charles Boyle, Earl of Orrery—hence the name
(Courtesy of J. M. Botibol, Esq.)

115

time : But whereas that is fixed, this outermost one is moveable, & by a particular and very curious Contrivance, is carried forwards or backwards in such manner, that the same hand, which by an equal motion, points to the minutes of the Equal Time upon the fixed Circle, points likewise to the minutes of the Solar Time, upon the moveable one ; and by comparing the divisions of these two Circles together, the difference between the Equal and Solar time, may at any time be seen.

" In the elevated part of ye Dialplate, there is cut an opening, through which appears a Silvered Plate which makes one revolution in 365 days 6 hours, & has the days of the month, the months of the Year, the signs of the Zodiac, & the Suns place in the Ecliptic, for each day in the Year engraved upon it. This annual Circle is pointed to, by two steel Indexes screwed to the Dialplate, set the distance of eleven divisions from each other ; against the one, which shews the days of the month according to the old Stile is VS, and against the other NS which marks the days according to the new Stile. Within the several Circles abovementioned, there is a smaller Plate, which makes but one revolution in four Years ; & shews the number of years it is after the Bissextile or Leap-year.

" In the middle of the hour Circle, directly under the center of the hourhand, is an opening cut in the Dialplate, through which appears a Plate, having the names of the days of the Week, & the Planet after which each day is called, engraved upon it ; This Plate makes one revolution in seven Days.

" The Size of the Annual Plate, not permitting the divisions which shew the days of the Month, to be of a size sufficient to render them distinct, at so great a distance as they are placed from the Eye, there is a square hole pierced in the Dialplate, under the minute Circle, thro' which is shewn the days of the months, as in a common Clock ; but with this peculiar and extraordinary Circumstance, that whereas in a common Clock, the day of the month requires to be set one day forward, in all those months which contain but thirty days, & three days at the end of Feby in this, there is no alteration ever required ; but it will always shew the true day, whether the months are of 30 or 31 days, or Feb^y: contains 28 or 29 days ; & consequently will always exactly agree with the days of the month, as shewn by the Annual Circle.

" The great Judgement shewn in the Contrivance, by wch the various Motions above described are performed, does great honour to that Celebrated Artist M^r. Thomas Tompion, by whom most of them were originally invented : & from the Improvements made (to the original Contrivances) in this Clock, and the very great accuracy, with which the whole Work is executed, it may justly be esteemed a most elegant & curious Piece of Workmanship."

Although from the last paragraph it appears that Tompion made several of these year equation timepieces of this type, there are only three at the present time recorded, the two in the possession of H.M. the King, and the Drayton example.

The table clock, Fig. 74, is another outstanding example of Tompion's work ; the movement having an elaborate mechanism with the *grande sonnerie* striking—the hours and quarters at each quarter, the quarters being chimed on three bells.[1] A feature of this particular *grande sonnerie* movement, which is but rarely found in other clocks fitted with this mechanism, is that one train does the double duty of striking the hours and chiming the quarters instead of the usual practice of two trains—one for each function. The movement is also fitted with a repeating action by which the hour is struck and the nearest quarter chimed at will on the pulling of a cord. In a period when the chief illuminants were candles and lamps and the only method of obtaining a light was with a tinder box, the necessity for some device to tell the time in the dark or in a dimly lighted room caused the invention of the repeating movement.[2]

Another unusual feature of this table clock is that the case has no door at the back ; the only method of obtaining access to the movement is by lifting off the case after unscrewing the bottom plate on to which the movement is fixed. Because of this construction the back plate is plain without engraving and the pendulum has of necessity to be held when the clock is moved. This last was accomplished by the hands of the two lower quadrant dials actuating levers which gripped the bob of the pendulum, *vide* Figs. 76 and 92. The upper quadrant dials are for the regulating of the pendulum and the " strike silent."

The two exceptional table clocks, both by Tompion, Figs. 78 and 89, also possess *grande sonnerie* striking and repeating movements of a similar type to the example just reviewed ; in fact the lay-out of the clock-work in all three movements differs only in detail. Every one of the movements displays an ordered progression of refinement of workmanship and improvement of design, which shows that Tompion did not make them at the same time. The first to be made appears to be Fig. 78, the second Fig. 89, and the third Fig. 74.

The example in the mercurial gilt case, Fig. 89, is unlike the other two in the one respect

---

[1]The clock with a quarter chiming movement chimes the quarters only and does not strike the hour at the quarter as well.

[2]Robert Hooke records in his *Diary* under date Friday, November 10th, 1676, that he was " At Tompions, told him of my new striking clock, to tell at any time howr and minute by sound." Edward Barlow and Daniel Quare are said to have been the inventors of the repeating mechanism, but the above entry suggests that Hooke also may have had a share in the invention.

that it has an alarm mechanism. The alarm is wound up by the hand belonging to the top right quadrant which in the other two clocks operates the "strike silent." In the alarm movement the "strike silent" is operated by a slide at the top of the dial.

The dials of these three clocks are nearly identical as regards the chased ornament and their general design. One difference is that the example with the alarm has Tompion's name engraved at the base of the dial, whereas in the other two clocks the name is on an engraved panel just below the slot of the pendulum indicator. This difference is due to the small dial of the alarm overlapping the name plate; the engraver therefore filled the panel with chased ornament and placed Tompion's name below.

The table clock, illustrated Fig. 80, has also *grande sonnerie* striking and a repeater movement. The design of the clockwork of this example shows a more advanced stage of development in comparison to the three earlier clocks just considered. Unlike the earlier examples with two trains, it has three trains—the going, the striking and the chiming, which last named action is carried out on six bells. The back plate, *vide* Fig. 82, has engraved at the base below the bob of the pendulum the number of the movement—217. This number places the date of the clock about 1690-95.

The two small circles at the top corners of the dial are for regulating the pendulum and the "strike and silent." The circle for the latter, which is on the right, has four positions for the arm, marked respectively

S | 6   N | 6   S | 1   N | 1

The first position allows the movement to strike and chime on the six bells. The second, the striking is stopped but the chiming persists. The third, the striking persists and the chiming is stopped. The fourth, both the striking and the chiming are stopped and the clock is silent.

A change that took place in certain of Tompion's table clocks of this period was that the dial plate altered its proportion from square to oblong; the presence of the regulating and "strike and silent" circles being the reason for this.

The case of this clock which is of veneered ebony with finely chased mounts, mercurial gilt, is of a type that Tompion adopted in the reign of William III for his most important clocks. The clock case-maker, like the cabinet-maker, overcame the difficulty of design by employing as decorative motifs architectural features such as pilasters, columns, entablatures, arches, pedestals, domes and urns. The set proportions of the classic orders of architecture were of great assistance in the designing of clock-cases and pieces of furniture in this period as they endowed such articles with the basis of good design. The clock-case illustrated shows to what degree its designer borrowed the proportions and features of classic architecture. The escutcheon with swags affixed to the dome was intended for the display of the coat of arms or crest of the owner and the low pedestal, upon which the Doric columns stand, contains a drawer. The figure surmounting the dome is a feature that Tompion especially favoured for the cases of his more important clocks, both long-case and table, *vide* Figs. 66, 73, 80 and 84.

The table clock in veneered tortoiseshell case, *vide* Fig. 84, possesses a movement—fitted with repeating action and *grande sonnerie* striking—of a similar type to that of the clock just described. It is, however, a partnership clock being the work of Tompion and his nephew Edward Banger. It has three trains and chimes on six bells and has the same "strike and silent" action as already described. The dial has now become arched so as to accommodate the elaborate calendar work that shows the date, the day of the week and the month. The design and quality of this clock shows a still further development of Tompion's technique; in fact it can be said that it is representative of the master's work at its best. Its date—the back plate is engraved with the number 436—is approximately the early years of Queen Anne's reign.

The design of the case, with its ogee curved dome tapering upwards to carry the pedestal upon which stands the figure, and its general proportions are excellent. The four metal urns and the continuous pedestal which appears in the front and the two sides of the case, endow the design with a pleasing architectural quality. Other features of the design are the widening of the case at the base, which gives a sense of stability, and the metal whorls of the scrolling sides answering to the two small dials. The scrolled sides and the metal mouldings give the case a French character. One other feature of this masterpiece of Tompion's is the mint state not only of the case, but of the movement. Such a condition could only have been brought about by the great care

118

Fig. 80. A TABLE CLOCK, with repeater movement and *grande sonnerie* striking on six bells, by Thomas Tompion. The case is of veneered ebony with mercurial gilt mounts. Total height 2 ft. 3 ins. *Temp.* 1690–95.
(*Collection of Mrs. Kroyer-Kielberg*)

119

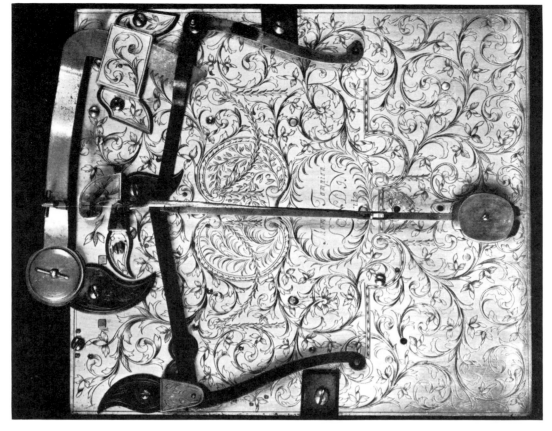

Figs. 81 and 82. DETAIL OF CLOCK illustrated Fig. 80, showing dial and engraved back plate with name and number 217

121

Fig. 83. DETAIL showing side view of case of clock
illustrated Fig. 84

the clock must have received from the hands of its various owners during its long life of over two hundred years.

The ambitious design of the cases of these two outstanding table clocks, of ebony and tortoiseshell, together with the superb quality of the craftsmanship of the gilded metal ornaments, indicates that both clocks originally must have been made to the order of two of Tompion's wealthy patrons.

An interesting feature concerning the cases is that the mount in the form of a frieze with two cupids and a satyr's mask decorating the pedestal of the ebony cased clock also appears on the rail below the door of the clock with tortoiseshell case. Tompion's case-maker (it would be of great interest to know something about this craftsman) must have had numerous stock moulds for all types of " Ornaments," which he used as occasion arose for the decoration of Tompion's clock-cases. For this reason the same ornaments will be found decorating various clocks. These case ornaments were undoubtedly designed to accord with Tompion's own wishes and ideas and in consequence they possess an individual character; the same remark also applies to the ornaments of Tompion's dials. It is possible that Tompion with his large output of clocks may have had his own case-makers' workshop or what is perhaps more likely he employed a firm of case-makers who worked for him alone.

The rich quality of the gilding of the case and dial ornaments and the dial plates is an outstanding feature of Tompion's clocks. This fact can be fully appreciated when a dial that possesses its original gilding is compared to one that has been regilt; the depth and richness of colour of the old gilding is absent in the modern work. Tompion also ornamented his table clock-cases with silver mounts, *vide* Tompion's bill quoted page 130.

Robert Hooke writes in his " Diary," under date Monday, January 29th, 1676. " To Garways. Met Sir Ch. Scarborough.[1] Taught him the way for the shell to turne about the Moon at the top of the clock and to show how the shadow hides the parts and spots of the Moon, advised him to have also a movable horizon, the way of both which I shewd Tompion next night." Tuesday, the following day, occurs the entry : " At Garaways directed

---

[1] Sir Charles Scarburgh (1616-1694), F.R.S., Physician to Charles II and to James II, Queen Mary and Prince George of Denmark.

Fig 84.   A TABLE CLOCK, with repeater movement and *grande sonnerie* striking on six bells, by Thomas Tompion and Edward Banger.   The case is of veneered tortoiseshell with mercurial gilt mounts and mouldings.   Total Height, 2 ft. 7 ins.   *Temp.* Queen Anne.

(Collection of S. E. Prestige, Esq.)

123

Tompion." This slight description of a piece of clockwork suggests that it referred to an astronomical clock.

Horologists, watch- and clock-makers in the time of Charles II came to delight in designing clockwork to carry out the most complicated motions. Clock movements fitted with perpetual calendars that made allowance for leap year, equation clocks that told the difference between solar time and mean time, astronomical clocks that indicated, apart from other motions, the position of the sun and moon in the zodiac and the altitude of the sun, the moon and the stars, were some of the remarkable achievements of this period.

Charles II, who delighted in the then new study of horology and the mechanic arts had a cabinet at Whitehall in which was displayed his collection of watches and clocks. John Evelyn records that on the 1st of November, 1660, he saw in " his Majesty's cabinet and closet of rarities ; . . . . . and, amongst the clocks, one that showed the rising and setting of the sun in the zodiac ; the sun represented by a face and rays of gold, upon an azure sky, observing the diurnal and annual motion, rising and setting behind a landscape of hills, the work of our famous Fromantil ; . . . . ."

It was due undoubtedly to the wealthy patronage of the King and the dilettante members of the nobility that the science of watch- and clock-making made such rapid strides in the late 17th century.

The remarkable astrolabe clock, Figs. 85-7, by Thomas Tompion is a product of this fertile age of the Restoration. The movement, in addition to showing the mean time in hours and minutes, shows the declination and position in the zodiac of the mean sun, the declination, position in the zodiac, age and phase of the moon, and the altitude and azimuth (when above the horizon) of the mean sun, the moon and a number of selected stars. The movement also indicates the position of the true or apparent sun in the zodiac as well as the date.

The dial plate, which measures $10\frac{1}{4}$ inches square, displays exquisite craftsmanship and perfection of design. It is mercurial gilt and so is the rotating fret with its scale of dates on its outer edge and the signs of the zodiac on the inner. The horizon is the line which demarcates the darker crescent shaped portion of the background of the dial, stained a deep

Fig. 85. A LONG-CASE ASTROLABE CLOCK by Thomas Tompion, the case veneered with olive wood and small panels of flowered marquetry.
Circa 1675-80.
(*Collection of S. E. Prestige, Esq.*)

125

blue; above the horizon line the background is stained an azure blue. The chapter circle, which shows twice twelve hours, the two inner circles, and the spandrel ornaments are of silver. The two pointers or arms are for the sun and moon respectively, each being identified by their respective signs affixed to the tips of the arms. The mean solar time in hours is shewn by the reading of the sun pointer upon the chapter circle and the minute hand rotating once in an hour gives the minutes of mean solar time. The moon arm indicates on the chapter

circle lunar time or the time which would be indicated by a moon dial.

The following is an interesting description of the way in which the dial registers the altitude and azimuth of the stars.

"The position of each of a number of the brighter stars is marked on the fret by a small star. As the fret slowly rotates clockwise a star initially, say, in the lower left-hand portion of the fret will slowly move up and cross the horizon. Its azimuth as it rises can be read off on the scale of azimuth lines, the

Fig. 86. DETAIL of dial of Astrolabe Clock illustrated Fig. 85. The chapter and the two inner circles and spandrel mounts are of silver and the dial-plate and the scroll fret are mercurial gilt.

Fig. 87.   DETAIL of Hood and Dial of Astrolabe Clock by Thomas Tompion, illustrated Fig. 85.
(*Collection of S. E. Prestige, Esq.*)

127

lowermost ends of which are numbered 10, 20, 30, etc. As the night progresses the star rises higher, and at any instant its altitude and azimuth can be read off on the fixed background scale. The star reaches its maximum altitude as it crosses the line joining the XII figure to the centre of rotation, and then its altitude decreases until it meets the horizon line and sets. The dial shows at a glance which stars are visible above the horizon at any instant. In the particular rotating fret of this clock only stars having a declination between about $+35°$ and $-24°$ are shown."[1]

The movement of the clock is of month duration; the winding is geared so as to allow the winding squares to be situated at the base of the dial. The movement is fitted with maintaining power so that in the process of winding the clock will not stop. This power is brought into action by a lever at the side of the movement and there are not the usual shutters over the winding holes (to remind one to pull the lever) as the winding squares project too far to permit the shutters to slide between them and the back of the dial plate. The date that Tompion produced this clock would appear to be about 1675-80.

The case is of particular interest, its design and general character being typical of the cabinet work of the time of Charles II. The panels on the door and base and the hood are veneered with a parquetry pattern formed of "oysters" of olive wood; the mouldings and borders are crossbanded with straight grained olive, and the leaves of the flowers in the central marquetry panel are stained green. The carved open pediment, centred by a basket of flowers, surmounting the cornice, is of unusual design and a rare feature in clocks of this period.

This clock with its dial of gold, silver and blue and its case of pale and dark olive wood veneers has a most striking and distinguished appearance. Unfortunately the name of Tompion's patron who gave the commission for the design and construction of this remarkable clock, is never likely to be known, as little or nothing can be discovered about the clock's past history.

The eight remarkable clocks — three long-case and five table — which have been described, show how swift was the progress of horological design in the hands of a master like Thomas Tompion with his two eminent assistants, George Graham and Edward Banger.

To sum up the outstanding features that occur in these eight clocks—one goes for three months without re-winding and is fitted with a perpetual calendar that makes allowance for leap year; another goes for one year without re-winding and the dial registers the difference between Equal Time or the time by the clock, and Apparent or Solar Time.

Fig. 88. A TABLE CLOCK in veneered ebony case of small size (10¾ in. high), with pull quarter movement by Thomas Tompion

(Collection of S. E. Prestige, Esq.)

---

[1] I am indebted to Mr. F. A. B. Ward for this description, and also for the other information that I have incorporated in the account of the movement of this astrolabe clock.

Of the five table clocks all have *grande sonnerie* and repeating movements. The three earliest clocks that date from the latter part of Charles II's reign are especially remarkable for the reason of the mature design and the elaborate nature of the clock-work at so early a date. The fifth table clock by Tompion and Banger displays Tompion's craftsmanship—no longer in the early experimental stages—at the highest state of perfection. And last there is the unique astrolabe clock with its many complicated motions which bears testimony to Tompion's creative genius.

Because so few of Tompion's bills have been published, the following interesting Royal bills for watches and clocks are quoted at length.

1693.   Delivred for Her Maj:tie service To The Rt Honble the Countess of Darby by Thomas Tompion.

May ye 8:th A Gold watch at twentythreepo 13s . . . . 23 : 13 :
Augt 16 A Spring Clock in a Tortoise Shell Case. . . . . . . 40 : 00 :
March ye 28 A large Moenth Clock a fine wallnut tree Case wth ye Diall plate Capitall & bases Gilt. . . . 25 : 00 :
September 26 for Cleaneing & Mending ye Queens quarter repeateing Spring Clock 1 : 05 :
October ye 15th for Cleaneing & Mending the Queens repeateing watch & a New glass & Lineing the Case . . . 0 : 15 :
_____
90 : 13 :
_____

Dessember ye 18th The perticullers Above Mentioned Amounteing to ye Sume of Ninty pounds Thirteen Shilings hath been received for Her Majtie us per me.

E. Derby.

The following are two further bills of Tompion's for watches and clocks for royal presents.

From Michas 1694 to Michas 1695
THOMAS TOMPION
Watch-maker
For Presents from his Maty to Algiers

For one repeating gold watch £70
For a gold Watch £23
For a silver Watch £11
For Presents from his Maty to Tripoli
For one repeating gold watch & 5 other gold Watches £231
From Michas 1697 to Michas 1698
Thomas Tompion Clockmaker
For presents from his Ma.ty to the Governmt. of Tunis
For 2 large gold watches in graved cases at £33 each £66
For a new spring repeating quarter clock an Ebony case and fine silver Ornaments £95
For a new spring clock with an Ebony case & silver Ornaments £75
For presents to the Governm.ts of Algiers and Tripoli formerly provided from ye Office of his Ma.ts Gr Wardrobe
For repairing the damage of 9 gold Watches and putting new outcases to the having been retayned att Portsmouth above two yeares £5

Undoubtedly, one of the reasons why these Royal gift watches were more expensive than the gold watch of Queen Mary was that they were repeating watches. A repeating watch was fitted with a spring, which when pressed caused a bell to strike the hours and quarters.

The prices of the two table clocks in ebony cases with silver mounts appear unduly costly as they represent at least several hundred pounds each of our present money. The cases of these two clocks were probably of the same high quality as the Tompion and Banger clock illustrated.

In the reign of William III, Tompion must have found the position of clockmaker to the court a very lucrative one. The high esteem in which he was held by his contemporaries, both as a watch- and clock-maker and also as a horologist, meant that he had but few competitors.

The facts concerning Tompion's life and career that the present writer has been able to gather together in this monograph are only too scant. Further research will provide more material for a biography of England's greatest watch- and clock-maker.

SIGNATURE OF THOMAS TOMPION
reproduced from his Will, 21st October, 1713

Fig. 89. A TABLE CLOCK with repeater movement and *grande sonnerie* striking by Thomas Tompion. The case is of metal
mercurial gilt with silver mounts. *Temp.* Charles II
This clock was the gift of King Charles II to Barbara, Countess of Castlemaine
(*Collection of The Duke of Grafton*)

132

CHAPTER VII
ENGLISH METAL-CASED TABLE CLOCKS OF THE SEVENTEENTH AND EIGHTEENTH CENTURIES

ENGLISH and Continental clocks of the 16th century were made usually with cases of copper or brass—mercurial gilt. This metal-cased clock went out of fashion in England in the 17th century, that is if the brass lantern clock is not included in the same category.

The cases of English table clocks dating from the last half of the 17th century, were seldom of any other material than wood, usually veneered with pear-wood ebonised, and a lesser number with ebony, walnut, olive-wood, king-wood, or tortoiseshell veneer. The veneered wooden case continued in favour for table clocks throughout the 18th century and during the latter part of the century mahogany and satin wood were substituted for walnut and olive.

The production of metal-cased clocks in the 17th and 18th centuries appears to have been of little account, that is, if the few known examples can be taken as any indication of the original output.

The metal case, owing to its indestructible nature, must have possessed a longer life than the wooden case. Also, apart from this, it did not become shabby or worn, and consequently was not readily discarded. For this reason the percentage of survivals must be high.

In considering the metal cases of table clocks, a distinction must be drawn between a case of metal construction and a wooden case

Fig. 90. A TABLE CLOCK in mercurial gilt metal case, with movement by Richard Fennell. Late 17th century
(*Collection of Major Sir John Prestige*)

overlaid with thin sheets of metal in the manner of French Boulle work.

An interesting point as regards these metal clock cases is the type of craftsman responsible for their construction. The smallness of their output suggests that their production was not a special trade, and that they must have been made by a metal worker of an associate craft. The watch-case-maker and the "clock-engraver" would appear to be the two most likely craftsmen.

The metal case of the table clock was usually mercurial gilt. Some cases were unornamented, the mouldings being the only relief, Fig. 90; others were decorated with cast mounts, and a third type with engraving, Fig. 95. The last two methods were used together, as in the exceptional clock case illustrated, Fig. 89, in which the silver mounts are in brilliant relief against the gold background of the mercurial gilt brass of the case.

A far more unusual type of metal case was one made of steel, similar to the example, Figs. 93 and 94. This rare and exquisite little clock—it is the work of Tompion and measures, with the handle, 7¾ ins. in height—has a case of which the body is of blued steel; the handle, basket top, frets and mouldings are mercurial gilt and the escutcheon to the keyhole of the door and the beading holding the glass are of silver.

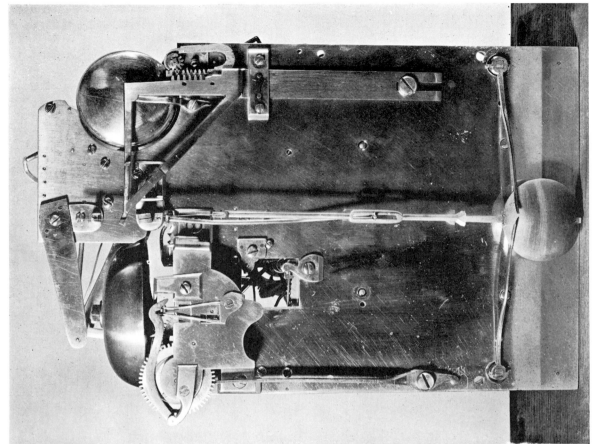

Fig. 92. DETAIL OF BACK PLATE of movement of clock illustrated Fig. 89, showing mechanism for regulating length of pendulum and the forked arms for holding it
(*Collection of the Institution of Civil Engineers*)

Fig. 91. DETAIL showing the back and side of the table clock illustrated Fig. 89. The open work panels are of cast silver

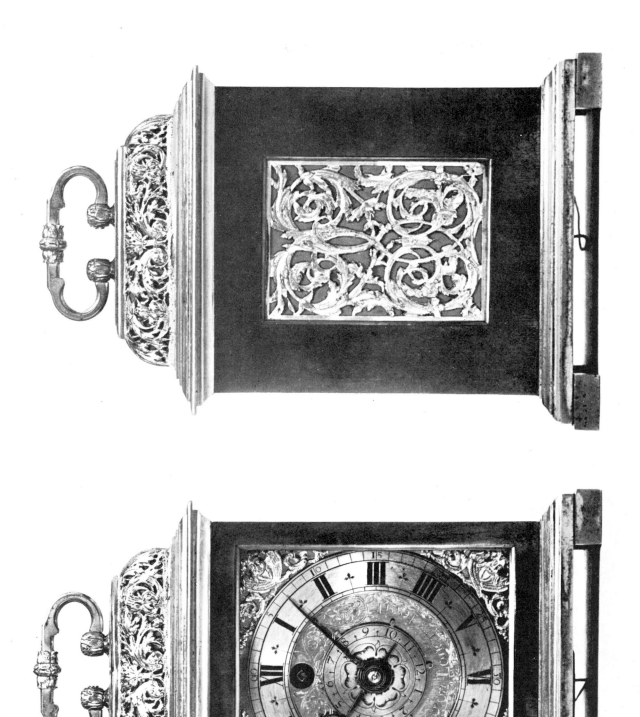

Fig. 93. A MINIATURE TABLE CLOCK with movement by Thomas Tompion and case of blued steel with basket top, frets and mouldings mercurial gilt. Height with handle 7¾ in. Late 17th century
(Collection of S. E. Prestige, Esq.)

Fig. 94. DETAIL showing back of clock, illustrated Fig. 93, with open work gilt fret panel

135

Unquestionably the choice of metal for the case of a table clock was not because of the strength or durability of the material, but a desire on the part of the maker to produce a special clock of an outstanding richness of effect. For this reason, these table clocks in the majority of instances may have been made to the special order of a wealthy customer. It is possible also that they were favoured by some English makers when executing an important commission for a foreign patron; the silver and gilt case answering to the taste of those countries such as Spain, Russia and Turkey, where bright and glittering objects were cared for.

In considering further the clocks illustrated, the example by Thomas Tompion, Fig. 89, apart from the beautiful case and dial, possesses a historic interest, as it was the gift of King Charles II to the famous Lady Castlemaine. It is through the family of the Dukes of Grafton

Fig. 96. A MUSICAL CLOCK, playing six tunes, by William Webster, Exchange Alley, London. The case is of metal mercurial gilt. *Circa* 1730
(*Collection of Major Sir John Prestige*)

Fig. 95. DETAIL showing the finely pierced frets and engraving decorating the side of clock illustrated Fig. 96

that the clock has descended; the first Duke being Lady Castlemaine's natural son by the King.

Unfortunately the clock is not intact, as in the 19th century, the fifth Duke of Grafton instructed the court clockmaker, Benjamin Lewis Vulliamy, to put the movement into repair. These instructions Vulliamy carried out by replacing Tompion's movement with one of his own. It is evident that Vulliamy realised the horological value of the Tompion movement, as he presented it in 1847 to the Institution of Civil Engineers, of which body he was a member. This act makes Vulliamy far more reprehensible than if he had destroyed the movement merely through ignorance of its importance. To-day, Tompion's divorced movement is under glass at the Institution of

Fig. 97. A MINIATURE TABLE CLOCK in mercurial gilt case with movement—30-hour striking—by Richard Peckover. 6⅜ in. in height. *Circa* 1740
(*Collection of S. E. Prestige, Esq.*)

(it measures with the handle 6⅜ ins. in height), which is illustrated in Fig. 97, is by Richard Peckover; it also has a mercurial gilt case. The spandrel ornaments are of silver, and the 30-hour movement is a pull quarter repeater on three bells. Very little is known of these two makers, Richard Fennell and Richard Peckover; the former was admitted a freeman to the Clockmakers' Company in 1679, and the latter's address was Change Alley, Cornhill.[1]

The table clock by William Webster, Fig. 96, is an imposing example of a musical clock in a metal gilt case. The mercurial gilding and the engraving of the unusual arabesque designs ornamenting the sides of the case are both of the highest quality. The pierced and engraved metal frets on the front and sides also display a fine craftsmanship.

There were several generations of the family of Webster at Exchange Alley, London. William Webster I, who was the maker of this clock, proclaimed that he was an apprentice and journeyman of Thomas Tompion, as on the death of this famous maker, he took the oppor-

[1] Cf., *Old Clocks and Watches and their Makers.* F. J. Britten.

Civil Engineers, Westminster, whilst the shimmering gold and silver case with its dial inscribed *Thomas Tompion* is on the drawing-room chimneypiece at the Duke of Grafton's home, Euston, Suffolk.

It is interesting to note the similarity of the design of the case of this clock with that of the ebony cased example, Fig. 74. Both cases possess handles of nearly identical design; mouldings of a similar section; considerable similarity in the fret panels decorating the sides and back and the same finials of tulip shape. On the Duke of Grafton's clock the mounts are of silver, whereas on the latter example they are of brass mercurial gilt.

The small table clock, Fig. 90, with its metal case in the style of the late 17th century, is by Richard Fennell. The case is mercurial gilt, and its bold mouldings make it a particular pleasing design. Another small table clock

Fig. 98. A TRAVELLING CLOCK, probably a ship's clock, with movement with a lever escapement with brass balance wheel by William Mason. Case of lacquered brass with bronzed frets. Mid-18th century
(*Courtesy of Malcolm Webster, Esq.*)

tunity of advertising in several of the newspapers his former connection with his late master.

> "On the 20th Instant Mr. Thomas Tompion noted for making all Sorts of the best Clocks and Watches, departed this Life. This is to certify all Persons of whatever Quality or Distinction, that WILLIAM WEBSTER, at the Dyal and Three Crowns in Exchange-Alley, London, served his Apprenticeship and lived as a Journey-man a considerable time with the said Mr. Tompion, and by his Industry and Care is fully acquainted with his Secrets in the said Art." [Cf., *The Englishman*, November 21st, 1713.]

The Daily Journal of August 14th, 1735, records that " Yesterday in the Afternoon died Mr. William Webster, a very eminent Watchmaker in Exchange-alley."

The metal-cased clock, Fig. 98, unlike the others illustrated, is not a table clock but a travelling clock. It is designed either to stand or to hang, the latter position when it was used travelling. It is unusual in the respect that instead of an ordinary suspension ring it has a gimbal, which is a ring working on two sets of pivots, thereby allowing the clock to remain in an upright position, however much the vehicle sways in which it is suspended.[1] This clock being designed for use whilst travelling has of necessity a balance wheel and not a pendulum, as the latter would not function properly unless the clock is standing perfectly steady. Very few English metal-cased travelling clocks with a balance wheel movement could have been made, judging from the small number of known examples. It would appear that in the 17th and 18th centuries the large travelling or coach watch, similar to the example illustrated in Fig. 99, was the most usual instrument for telling the time in coaches and carriages. Such watches were often made with a repeating movement and were fitted usually with an alarm ; two essential adjuncts to a travelling watch or clock, one to tell the hour in a dimly lit coach and the other to arouse the traveller from his bed in the early morning.

Another type of travelling clock—that could not have been used during the journey as it had a pendulum—was one made for the traveller to take with him on his travels and to unpack and set going when he arrived at an inn

for the night.[2] Such a clock was fitted with a travelling case or box, an alarm, and usually a repeating movement ; it was also of small size so that it would not take up much room in a trunk if the traveller was journeying by coach, or in a male or portmanteau if he rode on horseback. The majority of these pendulum travellers' clocks, that have survived, date from the 18th century, and have plain functional cases of lacquered brass, and they fit into wooden boxes with hinged lids.

It seems likely that the three small clocks, by Tompion, Fennell and Peckover, may have been superior travellers' clocks of this type, as all three are small in size and one has an alarm and another a repeating movement. If this is so, the original owner of the Tompion clock, with its case of blued steel, gilt and silver, must have possessed a particular taste to own so elegant a travelling clock.

Travellers' clocks had metal cases for the reason that it enabled them to withstand the rough usage and knocking about to which they were subjected in the course of their journeying.

In the 19th century the coach watch gave way to a metal-cased carriage clock with a balance wheel movement. Such balance or carriage clocks, as they were called, had leather cases and many of the earlier pre-Victorian examples displayed extremely fine craftsmanship. These clocks, although possessing gilt metal cases, are, however, outside the scope of the present account.

The mercurial gilt metal-cased table clock together with the traveller's clock in gilt case, were articles of luxury made for the wealthy. Such clocks were only occasionally produced in the 17th and 18th centuries and were never of an ordinary commercial type, as they had a quality in their execution and an individual character.

Possibly now that the subject of English metal-cased clocks has been broached and a few examples recorded, others may come to light and perhaps some from abroad.[3]

---

[1] It seems probable that this attachment to a travelling clock denotes that it was designed as a ship's clock.

[2] Journeys in the 17th and 18th centuries were long and tedious and according to Evelyn's *Diary* a stay of several days at one place before resuming a journey was not unusual when travelling on the Continent.

[3] Unfortunately the author has been unable to obtain a photograph of the small metal-cased clock which is said to have belonged to King William III. It has a movement by Daniel Quare, and the case is 6 ins. in height. An illustration of it appears in F. J. Britten's *Old Clocks and Watches and their Makers*.

Figs. 99 and 100. A LARGE COACH WATCH, 7 in. in diameter, in silver chased and pierced case, with 30-hour movement, pull string minute repeater by JOHN ELLICOTT, London. Case bears Hall-mark 1757.
(Collection of the late Percy Webster, Esq.)

John Ellicott (1706?–1772), the maker of the coach watch illustrated, calls for special comment because of the eminence he achieved not only as a watch- and clock-maker but also as a man of science. Ellicott does not appear to have been admitted to the Clockmakers' Company as his name is not mentioned in the Company's records. In 1736 he was elected a Fellow of the Royal Society and in 1752 he invented a compensated pendulum. He was appointed clock-maker to George III but it would seem that he attended to the Royal clocks in the previous reign, as on January 29th, 1759, the Lord Chamberlain's Office sent a request to the house-keeper at Kensington Palace to allow Mr. Ellicott, the Clock-maker, admission, so that he could put in order the Palace clocks as they were " very foul and out of repair."

Ellicott's father, John Ellicott I. was admitted to the Clockmakers' Company in 1696 ; he died in 1733 whilst he was acting as Renter Warden. That he was a maker of repute is indicated by the notice of his death in the *Daily Courant* of May 23rd, 1733.

" On Monday Night Mr. Elicoat, an eminent Watchmaker in Swithin's Alley, near the Royal Exchange, went to Bed seemingly in very good Health, and was found dead in his Bed next Morning."

In 1712 John Ellicott I.'s address was " Austin-Fryers, near Winchester Street," later he moved to Swithin's Alley, Royal Exchange, where after his death his son carried on his business. The firm of Ellicott continued from father to son for two further generations after the death of John Ellicott II.

The coach-watch, illustrated Figs. 99-100, by John Ellicott II., with its thirty-hour minute repeating movement, is of great rarity, as very few travelling or other watches of this period were minute repeaters. In this connection it is interesting to note that Robert Hooke, from a mention in his *Diary*, appears to have invented a minute repeating watch or clock as early as 1676. (Cf. footnote on page 117.)

BARBARA, COUNTESS OF CASTLEMAINE, afterwards Duchess of Cleveland, to whom the clock (illustrated in Fig. 89) was given by King Charles II. (*From the oil painting by Sir Peter Lely, in the collection of the Earl of Sandwich.*)

Fig. 101. DETAIL of Hood and Dial of long-case clock by John Fromanteel, illustrated Fig. 105. The chapter circle has every minute numbered and the name is inscribed at the base of dial plate. Three train movement with maintaining power. *Circa* 1675

(*Collection of Major Sir John Prestige*)

CHAPTER VIII
OTHER ENGLISH CLOCKMAKERS OF THE SEVENTEENTH CENTURY

JOHN EVELYN records in his diary for May 2nd, 1661 : " I return'd by Fromantil's, the famous clock-maker, to see some pendules, Monsieur Zulichem being with us." " Pendules " refers to the new clocks which were fitted with pendulums ; an invention of this period of outstanding horological importance. The equal swing of the pendulum gave to the clock a far greater accuracy in time-keeping and the pendulum also allowed for adjustment to counteract changes in temperature. The mention by Evelyn of Monsieur Zulichem is of especial interest, as this personage was Christiaan Huygens (1629–95), the celebrated Dutch mathematician and a Fellow of the Royal Society and " inventor of the pendule clock."

" Fromantil's " refers to the firm of clockmakers which was founded by Ahasuerus Fromanteel [I], a craftsman of Dutch descent, who was made a freeman of the Clockmakers' Company in 1632.[1] In 1655, Ahasuerus [II] was admitted to the freedom of the Company. Ahasuerus [III] and a John Fromanteel were admitted in 1663 but what relationship they bore to Ahasuerus [I] and [II] it has not been possible to trace. Unquestionably the Fromanteels were a large family and many of the

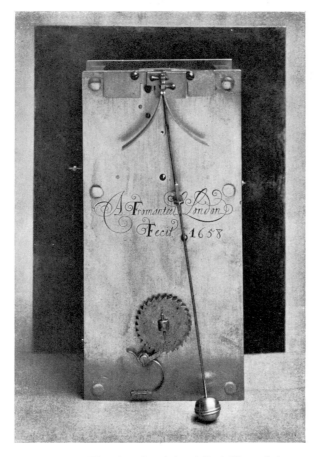

Fig. 102. The signed and dated Back Plate of the earliest English recorded pendulum clock
(*Collection of Major Sir John Prestige.*)

members worked together in the family firm of watch- and clock - makers. There was also a branch of the family working in Amsterdam.

It appears that the credit for the introduction of the pendulum into England is due to the Fromanteels.

" There is lately a way found out for making of clocks that go exact and keep equaller time then any now made without this Regulater (examined and proved before his Highness the Lord Protector, and by such Doctors whose knowledge and learning is without exception) and are not subject to alter by change of weather, as others are, and may be made to go a week, or a moneth, or a year, with once winding up, as well as those that are wound up every day, and keep time as well ; and is very excellent for all House clocks that go either with Springs or Waights : And also Steeple Clocks that are most subject to differ by change of weather. Made by *Ahasuerus Fromanteel*, who made the first that were in *England* : You may have them at his house on the Bankside in *Mosses* Alley, *Southwark*, and at the sign of the Maremaid in *Loathbury*, near *Bartholomew* lane end *London*." (*Mercurius Politicus*, October 21st–28th, 1658.)

The Fromanteels' connection with Holland gave them an advantage over other English clock-makers in obtaining particulars of the new pendulum clocks, for which there was a ready sale in England owing to their greater reliability.

Huygens assigned his rights in the invention of a pendulum clock to Saloman Coster, a clock-maker of the Hague, who was granted a patent in 1657 for its manufacture. An agreement between Saloman Coster and John

---

[1] This last named statement is made by numerous writers, but in Octavius Morgan's *List of Members of the Clockmakers' Company* (*Archæological Journal*, vol. XL, 1883), there is no reference of Ahasuerus [I] being admitted to the Company in 1632. He was admitted to the Blacksmiths' Company in 1630, prior to the formation of the Clockmakers' Company in 1631. Cf. *Some Account of the Worshipful Company of Clockmakers*, 1881.

Fig. 103. DETAIL of movement of Clock, illustrated Fig. 102, showing the going barrel and the square pillars

Fromanteel, dated September 3rd, 1657 (which is within four months of Coster's obtaining his patent) was discovered by Dr. Vollgraff in the municipal archives at the Hague. By this agreement Coster takes John Fromanteel into his service until May 1st, 1658 ; an arrangement which clearly shows that the Fromanteels were alive to the importance of the new pendulum clock and lost no time in sending one of the younger members of their family to Holland to learn its construction.[1]

[1] Cf. *The Evolution of Clockwork*. By J. Drummond Robertson, 1931.

The Fromanteels were accordingly in the position to advertise the making of clocks with " this Regulater " in October, 1658, after John Fromanteel's return to England. The fact that Huygens visited Fromanteel's shop with Evelyn suggests his approval of Fromanteel's work.

It would seem improbable that one of the actual clocks which Fromanteel advertises, " You may have them at his house on the Bank-side in *Mossess* Alley, *Southwark*, . . . " should still be in existence, but there is little doubt that the clock illustrated in Figs. 102–104 is such an example, for on the back plate is inscribed—*A Fromanteel London Fecit* 1658.

This clock has only recently been discovered and unfortunately when found it had been converted to an anchor escapement ; its original case had gone and only fragments of the dial plate remained. These last, however, were sufficient to show the position of the original name plate, and also that it was of segmental shape. Attempts to restore the fragmentary state of the original dial plate proved unsuccessful. Fortunately the interesting and finely wrought hands were found intact and in perfect condition. The replacement of the crown wheel escapement according to its original design was made possible by the fact that the pinion of the contrate wheel was the original and the marks on it clearly determined the position of this wheel in relation to the escape wheel, thereby giving its size. The accurate restoration of the potence and the cocks was rendered possible owing to the plates showing staining where the original parts had been fitted prior to the anchor escapement. Another guide was the holes of the original steady pins as well as the screw holes with their original threads which remained in the plates.

This clock shows in its design a combination of both English and Dutch practice and is the English counterpart of a clock in the Rijks Museum, signed and dated—*SAMUEL COS-TER—HAGHE met privilege* 1657.[2]

The Dutch design of the going barrel and the coarse square pillars should be noticed, *vide* Fig. 103. Unlike the Dutch this movement is designed to be seated on the base of the case instead of being hung on a hinged dial—the

[2] This clock, which was made in the same year that Coster was granted his patent for the making of pendulum clocks, was discovered by the late Mr. Drummond Robertson on a visit to the Rijks Museum and he illustrated and described it in his authoritative book *The Evolution of Clockwork*. 1931.

Dutch practice, and it is of 8-day duration and not 30 hours. Other English features are the hooked pillars and dial feet instead of the common pins. This movement, so far as the present writer is aware, is the earliest example known of this 17th century English method of holding the parts together.

The new dial with its matted gilt ground has been copied to be in keeping and the fine execution of the chapter circle is an interesting example of modern craftsmanship reproducing the old.

Ahasuerus [III] and John Fromanteel appear to have been the leading members of the Fromanteel firm in the time of Charles II, judging by the list of their apprentices and the number of extant clocks, both long-case and table, that bear their names.

An example of a long-case clock by John Fromanteel is illustrated in Fig. 105; it has several unusual features, apart from the fact that the movement does not adhere to the normal design of contemporary movements. The dial is inscribed at the base *Johannes Fromanteel Londoni fecit.* and each minute is numbered, the gilding is original and also the hands, *vide* Fig. 101 The fixing of the movement in the case is by a system of metal brackets in place of a seat board. The pallets are unusual in shape although normal in their function. The clock strikes the hours and quarters, the former on a chord of four bells, four hammers being on a single arbour, *vide* Fig. 106. The quarters are "ting-tang" on two additional bells; three trains are employed. The front plate of the movement is divided into three sections enabling any of the trains to be withdrawn separately for cleaning or repair. The arrangement is so good that it is surprising it was not adopted by later makers.

The pendulum vibrates 48 beats to the minute instead of 60, and is therefore approximately 60 inches in length instead of the normal 39 inches. It is interesting to note that in spite of the oft-repeated statement that all second and a quarter clocks have the second circle divided into 48 divisions instead of 60, it is in this case contradicted; the seconds dial, which is without doubt original and unaltered, having the usual 60 divisions. The length of the pendulum is regulated by a large milled nut, *vide* Fig. 106. This same method of pendulum adjustment is also to be found on two other clocks by John Fromanteel, which

are engraved with the years 1679 and 1681 respectively—the dates of their presentation to the Dutch Church in Austin Friars.

All the clockwork is entirely original and shows considerable technical knowledge at such an early period as 1675-80 which is the approximate date of this clock. The case is of the Charles II style, with small raised panels, but instead of being veneered with ebony—the more usual treatment for these early cases—it is of walnut veneer. The pediment and its entablature surmounting the hood are singularly correct in design. The deep plinth has since been removed, as it was not original to the case, being probably added in the 18th century, when the upward sliding hood was altered to a door. The replacement of this plinth by one of normal height has restored the case to its original proportion.

The following contemporary description is of a Fromanteel table clock with a case of the Dutch type which was favoured by the Fromanteels in the early years of Charles II reign.

" Stolen from Mr. *Chute's* house, the upper end of *Bedford-Row*, near *Grays Inn*, on Saturday the 29th of *June* last, between 10 and 11 at night, a large old heavy Pendulum Table-Clock, made by *Fromantle*, and his name engraven on the back plate, a little Silver Cherubs-head at each corner of the Dyal Plate, fixt in

Fig. 104. DETAIL showing the finely wrought hands and the modern dial of the clock illustrated Fig. 102

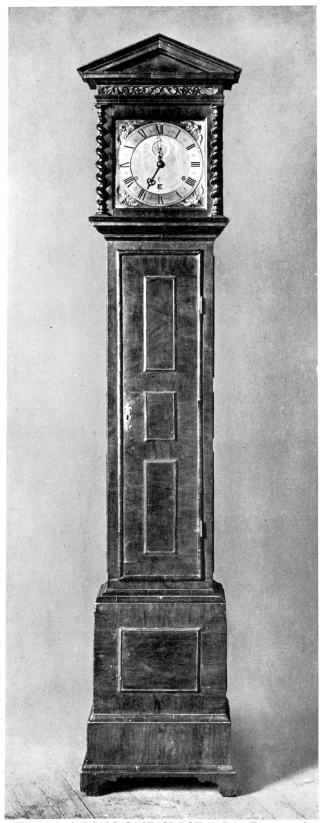

Fig. 105. A LONG-CASE CLOCK by John Fromanteel, three train movement, striking hours and quarters and with one and a quarter seconds pendulum. Veneered walnut case.
Circa 1675 (*Collection of Major Sir John Prestige*)

an Ebony Case of about a foot square, made in the form of a house, with a brass Urn at the top of each corner, and a Cupolo with a Cupid upon the top of it of brass gilt. (Cf. *The Post Man.* June 29, 1700.)

Another famous 17th century watch- and clock-maker, contemporary with the Fromanteels, was Edward East. An unusual example of this master's work is the night clock in long-case illustrated in Figs. 107 and 108. The movement is designed so that the light of a lamp placed at the back will shine through the piercing of the numerals of the dial, thereby telling the hours and quarters. (Cf. Fig. 108, where it will be seen the quarters are shown by the Roman numerals.) The design of the motion work controlling the moving circle in which the hours are cut is ingenious, and displays the inventive mind of its eminent maker. An outstanding feature of this clock is the engraved dial with the graceful design in the Dutch manner, composed of flowers and leaves and the elegant lettering *Edwardus East Londoni*. The case is typical of Charles II craftsmanship, being veneered with olive and walnut woods and decorated with " floured " panels " fine inlaid."

Night clocks appear to have been an innovation in the time of Charles II. Samuel Pepys alludes to one.

" After dinner to White Hall, and there met Mr. Pierce, and he showed me the Queen's bed-chamber, with her clock by her bedside, wherein a lamp burns that tells her the time of the night at any time." (June 24th, 1664.)

Apart from this long-case night clock there is extant a table night clock also by Edward East.[1]

In an account dated June 23, 1664, for clocks and watches " Delivered to his grace the Duke cf Richmond by James East Watchmaker " there appears an item for " A pendilum clocke to goe 8 dayes wth a lampe to shew the houre of the Night £45." The high cost suggests that this clock must have been something exceptional.

The following are further interesting items from this bill of James East:

June ye 23th 1664
  A large gold watch at the same time
  y^t shewes the day of the moneth   .. 22 : 00 : 00
A pendilum clocke   .. 05 : 00 : 00

---

[1] Illustrated *The Dictionary of English Furniture*, Macquoid and Edwards. 1924.

A large gold watch with two chaines
and two strings shewing the minutes .. 02 : 00 : 00
May 23ʰ 1672
ffor mending 3 pendilum Clockes one
silver clocke and two watches being
very much out of order .. 08 : 00 : 00
A sun diall and a moone diall .. 02 : 10 : 00
Altering a pendilum Clocke and to
make it goe in a ship .. 04 : 00 : 00

It would be interesting to know what was the alteration to a pendulum clock that made it go on board ship. In the last half of the 17th century this problem occupied the minds of several scientists, prominent amongst whom were Christiaan Huygens and Lord Kincardine [16 ? — 1681].

James East is mentioned in a warrant, dated April 4th, 1662, in which it is ordered that he should be sworn in as clockmaker to the Queen. It is possible that James worked with Edward East, who in all likelihood was a near relative. Another member of the East family who has not yet been recorded is "Nath East Clockmaker." In the Royal Wardrobe Accounts his name appears in connection with the following: "For Cleaning and mending the Great Wardrobe Clocke for 3 whole yeares past ending att Michas 1670 att 10s per Ann. £1-10-0."

Another clock by Edward East is the example, Fig. 109, with a weight-driven movement with a short bob pendulum and a hanging wall case of architectural character. This design of a weight-driven wall clock declined in favour when the two important improvements of the

long pendulum, known as the Royal pendulum, and the anchor escapement were invented in the early part of Charles II reign. The accuracy as a time-keeper of the long pendulum weight-driven movement was the cause of the popularity of the long-case clock, the long-case of which originated from the necessity to afford protection, first to the weights and then to the pendulum, as the earliest long-cases housed movements similar to that of the hanging wall clock illustrated with a bob pendulum.

Edward East, the famous watch and clock - maker, was watchmaker to Charles I. He was one of the ten original members of the Company of Clockmakers at its incorporation in 1632. During 1639 and 1640 he was renter warden, and in 1645 he was elected master. He was again master in 1652. He occupied the position of treasurer to the company in 1687 and was the only member to hold this office, which also ceased at his death.[1] In 1662 he was appointed "Chief Clockmaker and Keeper of the Privy Clocks."

The following advertisement of the first year of the Restoration mentions Mr. East.

"A large Knot of Diamonds set in Gold with a Hook in the form of such as men weare upon Breeches and a small Gold Chain thereunto affixed, was lost on Thursday the 29th of August, in or about the Cock Pit Play house in Drury Lane. This jewell is well known to very many persons of Quality at Court, and to divers Citizens. If any such be offered to Sale or Pawn,

Fig. 105. DETAIL of 8-day movement of long-case clock by John Fromanteel, illustrated Fig. 105. The four bells with the hammers on the one arbour are for striking the hours. The large circular headed nut is for regulating the pendulum

[1] Cf. *Some account of the Worshipful Company of Clockmakers,* 1881.

147

Fig. 107. A NIGHT CLOCK, by EDWARD EAST.
Case veneered with walnut and olive and decorated
with panels of floral marquetry of coloured woods.
Temp. Charles II
(*Collection of J. S. Sykes, Esq.*)

whoever stops it and gives notice thereof to Mr. East,
a Watchmaker, near St. Dunstan's Church in Fleet
Street shall receive five pounds and very many thanks.
(Cf. *Kingdom's Intelligencer.* August 26th–September
2nd, 1661.)

The fact that the lost jewel was well known

suggests that it may have belonged to King
Charles II.

A family of famous watch- and clock-makers
of the time of Charles II was that of Knibb.
The eldest member of the family was Samuel
Knibb, the maker of the clock illustrated in
Fig. 110. This maker's first address was at
Newport Pagnell and afterwards London, where
he was admitted to the Clockmakers' Company
in 1663.

The table clock illustrated by this master is
an interesting example being of a date probably
about 1670. Its noteworthy and early features
are the finely engraved and gilt dial plate, with
a floral design in the Dutch tradition, and the
plain back plate with the latches, which it was
customary to fit on the front plate, *vide* Fig. 111.

If it had been intended to engrave the back
plate with a design as was customary in clocks
of a slightly later date, then the latches would
have interfered with the pattern and in consequence this position for them would have
been unsuitable. It will be noticed that
on the plain back plate they become in themselves a decorative feature. The little engraved
ornament that the engraver allowed to appear
at the back of the movement was confined to
the outside locking plate and to the two cocks
and the scrolled lettering of the inscription
Samuel Knibb Londini fecit ; the lettering being
designed to follow the arc of the pendulum.
This clock strikes the coming hour on a small
bell at the half hour.

Two members of the next generation of the
Knibb family, were Joseph and John, the sons
of Thomas Knibb of Claydon, Oxfordshire.
The relationship that they bore to Samuel has
not been traced, possibly Samuel was brother
to Thomas and therefore their uncle. Joseph
and John Knibb worked together as clockmakers at Oxford until about 1670, when Joseph,
the elder brother, came to London, and was
admitted to the freedom of the Clockmakers'
Company in that year. John remained behind
and followed his trade of watch- and clock-
maker and in 1700 became Mayor of Oxford.[1]

Joseph in London built up a flourishing trade
and numbered amongst his patrons Charles II
and many members of the Court. The two
following advertisements give two of Knibb's
addresses and also an idea of his stock-in-trade.

" Joseph Knibb, Clockmaker, at the Dial at Serjeant's
Inn Gate, is now removed into Suffolk Street near

---

[1] Cf. *Johannes Knibb Oxoniae Fecit.* Article by John James in
Antique Collector. August, 1936.

Fig. 108. DETAIL showing the design and the fine execution of the engraved decoration on the dial of night clock
by Edward East, illustrated Fig. 107
(*Collection of J. S. Sykes, Esq.*)

149

Fig. 109.   A WALL CLOCK with weight-driven movement and bob pendulum, gilt dial plate inscribed
Edwardus East Londoni in bottom spandrels.   *Circa* 1670
(Courtesy of J. M. Botibol, Esq.)

151

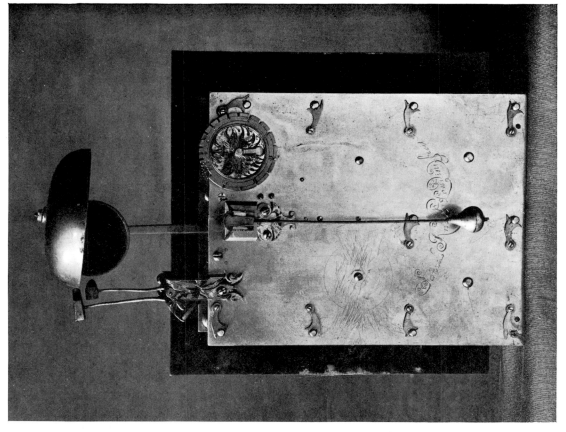

Figs. 110 and 111. A TABLE CLOCK by Samuel Knibb, London, with engraved and gilt dial plate. Name inscribed on back plate. Movement strikes the coming hour on a small bell at the half hour. *Circa* 1670
(Collection of Robert Norman Shaw, Esq.)

Fig. 112.   DETAIL of Hood and Dial of Long-case Clock by John Knibb, Oxon.,
illustrated Fig. 115
(*Courtesy of J. M. Botibol, Esq.*)

His invention of the striking mechanism according to Roman notation, was occasionally introduced by him as a special feature into the movements of both his long-case and table clocks; to-day the table clock with this original system of striking is much rarer than the long-case, as only a few specimens are known.

Towards the end of his career Joseph Knibb appeared to have left London and went to Handslope in Buckinghamshire as his later clocks are signed — *Joseph Knibb at Hanslop*. No evidence exists to say when this change took place, possibly the sale of his clocks which he advertised in 1697 was the disposal sale of his stock-in-trade prior to leaving for the country. Joseph Knibb died in 1711-12.

The clocks of John Knibb although exhibiting a high standard of craftsmanship and finish were a little more conservative in character and therefore were not so distinguished in the design of the dial plate and its ornaments as were the more fashionable London clocks of Joseph.

Charing-cross, where he has good conveniency to serve Customers with Clocks and Watches." (Cf. *The London Gazette.* October 2nd-October 5th, 1693.)

" At the Clock Dyal in Suffolk-street near Charing-Cross, on Monday the 26th instant, will begin the Sale of a great Parcel of very good Pendulum Clocks, made by Joseph Knibb ; some do go a year, some a quarter of a year, some a month, some a week, and some 30 hours ; some are Table Clocks, some Repeat themselves, and some by pulling Repeat the Hours and Quarters : They are made and to be sold by Joseph Knibb at his House at the Dyal in Suffolk-street aforementioned, where the sale will continue until Whitsuntide, unless all be sold sooner. There are also some Watches to be then and there sold, a good Penny-worths. (Cf. *The London Gazette.* April 22nd-April 26th, 1697.)

The clocks of Joseph Knibb apart from the distinctive design and fine craftsmanship of the clockwork, were particularly noteworthy for the elegance of the dials and hands.

The long-case clock, illustrated in Figs. 112 and 115, is typical of the design and craftsmanship of John Knibb. The case betrays no provincial characteristics in its design ; its excellent proportions and its simple ornamentation in the form of mouldings, fret and spiral turned columns, could not be improved upon. The original and " untouched " state of the movement and case of this example is exceptional for a 17th century clock ; it must have been for many generations in one family and in one house to account for such a state of preservation.

In the third generation of the Knibb family there was Peter Knibb who was apprenticed to Joseph and was admitted to the Clockmakers' Company in 1677. In 1693 Edward Knibb was also apprenticed to Joseph and later in 1710 Joseph Knibb [II] became apprenticed to

154

Martin Jackson. Neither of these last two members of the Knibb family, Edward and Joseph [II], were made free of the Clockmakers' Company, which suggests that after they had learnt their trade in London, they went to work in the provinces probably in their native towns.

An early clock by Samuel Knibb is a great rarity; both long-case and table clocks by Joseph and John Knibb are fairly numerous, whilst the later and more ordinary clocks by Peter Knibb are only occasionally to be seen.

John Ebsworth, the maker of the clock illustrated Figs. 113 and 114, was a contemporary of Joseph Knibb. He and Christopher Ebsworth, probably his younger brother, were both apprenticed to Richard Ames in 1657 and 1662 respectively. In 1665 John was admitted to the Clockmakers' Company and became Master in 1697. In his time, therefore, he was held in high repute, but according to opinion ruling to-day his clocks, although of character and distinction, rank below those of such masters as Tompion, Graham, East and Joseph Knibb.

The Ebsworth clock illustrated has a silver skeleton chapter circle with silver spandrel ornaments of the pattern that came after the winged cherub's head. This later ornament, which is associated with a date of about 1690, is somewhat unusual on a dial plate, the design which appears at least a decade earlier. The case is veneered with a parquetry of olive wood decorated with geometrical inlaid stars of a light coloured wood. It is also of an early type, but this, as already commented upon, is no guide to the date it was made, owing to the conservatism of the case-maker.

The maker, John Martin, of the table clock illustrated in Fig. 116, also belongs to the Charles II school of clockmakers. He was admitted to the Clockmakers' Company in 1679. In 1682 he was fined

by the Company for "undue taking and bindeing of apprentices" a misdemeanour that suggests his trade was prospering. The distinctive inlaid case of the clock illustrated would appear to have been especially favoured by the case-maker responsible for its production, as there are recorded over half a dozen cases of a similar type several of which contain movements by John Martin.

The table clock, Fig. 117, in ebonised case with gilt mounts, is by the well-known clock-maker Christopher Gould. This maker was admitted a Brother to the Clockmakers' Company in 1682, and was termed a "Great Clockmaker," which indicated that prior to his admission he had exercised his trade as a master. In 1713, Gould was chosen Beadle to the Company, which post he held until his death in 1718.

Fig. 113. DETAIL of Hood and Dial of Long-case Clock by John Ebsworth, with silver skeleton chapter circle and spandrel ornaments, illustrated Fig. 114

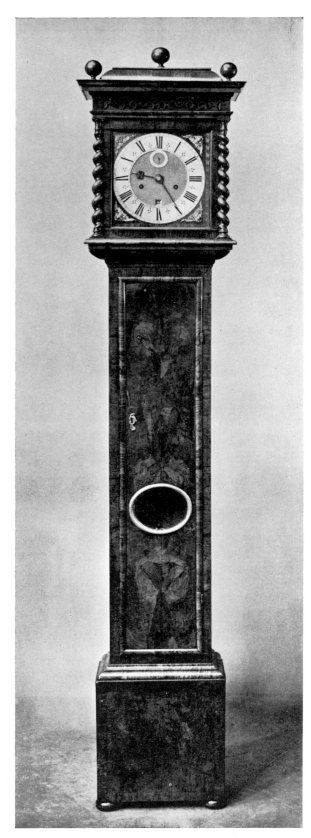

Fig. 114. A LONG-CASE CLOCK with 8-day movement by John Ebsworth. Case of olive wood parquetry.
Circa 1685

Fig. 115. A LONG-CASE CLOCK with 8-day movement by John Knibb, Oxon. Veneered walnut case
Circa 1680
(*Courtesy of J. M. Botibol, Esq.*)

156

The following advertisement concerning Gould and a lost clock gives the address of his premises :

"Lost, being miscarried betwixt North-hall and London, above 9 months since, a Table repeating Clock, in an ordinary black case, with slight Brass Work, the name forgot ; it was sent to London in a very strong Wainscot Box, directed to Chr. Gould Clockmaker without Moore-gate, if it hath come to any Workmans hand to mend, or any person can give an account of it so that the right owner may have it again, send word to the said Gould at his Shop next door to the Amsterdam Coffee-house behind the Royal Exchange, you shall have 10s. Reward.

(Cf. *The Post Man.* October 14-16. 1701.)

In 1706 Gould was declared bankrupt[1] and from this time to his death he appears to have suffered misfortune. Evidence of this is to be found in a petition to obtain for him the position of ale taster.

SIR, Your Vote and interest is humbly desired for CHRISTOPHER GOULD, Citizen and Clock-Maker, who hath many Years carried on a Considerable Trade, and lived in good Reputation, and is on the Livery, (but is now, by Losses and Misfortunes, with a numerous Family of Children, reduced to a very Low Condition) to be Ale-Conner in the Room of Mr. Joseph Swaffeild, Deceas'd. . . . (Cf. The *Daily Courant*, May 26th, 1714.)

There are numerous clocks extant, both long-case and table, made by Christopher Gould ; many of them have rather showy cases and the quality of the clock-work is not of a high order.

Daniel Quare was a celebrated watch- and clock-maker and belonged to the same rank as his famous contemporary Thomas Tompion. He was born in 1649[2] and was admitted, like Tompion and Gould, to the Clockmakers' Company as a Brother, being also called a

"Great Clockmaker." His admission was in 1671 and he was chosen on the Court of Assistants in 1697 and from 1705 to 1707 he was Warden and in 1708 he became Master.

Quare invented the repeating mechanism to watches, by which the wearer was able to tell the time in the dark by pressing a spring, which caused the watch to repeat the nearest hour and quarter. The Rev. Edward Barlow also invented, independently of Quare, a similar mechanism for which he applied for a patent. The Clockmakers' Company petitioned the King in Council against the grant of this monopoly to Barlow and at the hearing of the case, which took place in March, 1687, the Council having tested both Barlow's and Quare's repeating watches, gave preference to the latter and therefore the patent was refused.

Fig. 116. A TABLE CLOCK by John Martin, in inlaid case. *Circa* 1680

[1] Cf. *The Post Man*, October 31st, 1706.

[2] The year of Quare's birth is mentioned by several modern writers as 1649 ; no authority appears, however, to be cited for this date. In Octavius Morgan's *List of Members of the Clockmakers' Company* (*Archæological Journal*, Vol. XL, 1883) against Daniel Quare's name is written : "æt 92 *ob* 1724." If he was 92 when he died, this makes the year of his birth 1632.

Fig. 117. A TABLE CLOCK, by CHRISTOPHER GOULD, in ebonised veneered pear-wood case. Late 17th century

(*Collection of J. S. Sykes, Esq*)

Quare was appointed Clock-maker to George I. His two addresses, that so far have been identified from contemporary advertisements for lost watches, are St. Martin's-le-Grand and the King's Arms, Exchange Alley.

A celebrated clock by Quare is the long-case clock, with year movement, which stands in the corner of King William III's bedroom at Hampton Court Palace. The base of the clock is supported on a decorated gilt metal plinth and the hood is surmounted by a female figure of gilt metal with four *amorini* below situated at the corners of the hood.

Quare's clocks, of which a large number, both long-case and table, are extant, exhibit a greater variety, as regards the design and quality of the clockwork, than those of any other English maker. The reason for this wide divergency in design and quality may have been due to Quare's large export trade in watches and clocks with the continent. In order to cope with the many orders he received, he placed the making of clock movements, especially those that were for export, with chamber masters. Such outside work was therefore not produced under his supervision as in the case of his best

clocks, both long-case and table, which were made by his journeymen and apprentices in his own workshop.

Another solution to account for the variety in Quare's productions is that the inferior clocks which bear his name were contemporary forgeries. This suggestion, however, appears less likely than when his trade was flourishing he bought the clock movements of various chamber masters and after adding his name he sold them as his own. The table clock, Fig. 118, is an example from Quare's own workshop; it is of the highest quality both as regards the clockwork and the dial with its chased ornaments and mercurial gilding.

The following advertisement for a 17th century burglar alarm mentions Quare as both the maker and the seller.

"*Whereas* John Tizack *of* London, *Merchant, has Invented a Night Engine, which being set in a convenient place of any House, may prevent Thieves from breaking*

Fig. 118. A TABLE CLOCK, by DANIEL QUARE. The metal mounts are finely chased and mercurial gilt; the movement and dial are numbered 39. *Circa* 1715

(*Collection of S. E. Prestige, Esq.*)

in and surprising the Inhabitants, whereby many Robberies will be prevented : And has obtained of Their Majesties a Patent for the making the said Engine for the Kingdoms of England *and* Ireland. *These are therefore to give notice, that the said* John Tizack *has Licensed* Daniel Quare *in* Exchange-Alley, *and* Francis Stamper *at the* Golden-Ball *in* Lombard-street, London, *Clock-makers, to make and sell the same, and where they may be had at reasonable Rates.*

(Cf. *The London Gazette.* October 1.-4. 1694.)

Quare was a staunch Quaker, and it is said he refused the appointment of Royal clockmaker, when first it was offered to him, owing to his objection to the oath of allegiance. The following notice is evidence of his peaceful character—instead of prosecuting a thief he promises him a reward.

"Whereas Jos. Wheeler, Brushmaker by Trade, took away from Daniel Quare, Watchmaker in Exchange-Alley, London, Money and Bills of Value ; if any Person can secure him, so as he may be brought to the said D. Quare, he shall have 10 L Reward; but if he surrenders himself with the said Money and Bills before the 7th of May, 1709, he shall be allow'd 20 L.— Daniel Quare."

(Cf. *The Daily Courant,* May 2, 1709.)

Towards the end of his career Quare took into partnership Stephen Horseman who originally had been his apprentice. Horseman, after serving his seven years' apprenticeship, was admitted to the Clockmakers' Company in 1709. The clocks of the partnership were signed with both names usually—*Dan Quare and Ste Horseman.*

"Lost in the Post Office going from Amsterdam to Mantua, a GOLD MINUTE WATCH, made by Daniel Quare, No. 4602. The case chased all over with fine figures on the bottom. Whoever brings it to Daniel Quare and Stephen Horseman, Watchmakers, in Exchange Alley, London . . ."

(Cf. *The Daily Courant,* January 30, 1720.)

Fig. 119. A MINIATURE CLOCK in ebonised case with silver mounts and dial, by WILLIAM WEBSTER. Height 8 in. *Circa* 1720

(Collection of Lord Plender, G.B.E.)

In 1724 Daniel Quare died and the two following notices of his death show that this Quaker clock-maker achieved in his time international fame.

"Last Week dy'd *Daniel Quare*, Watch-maker in Exchange-Alley, who was famous both here and at Foreign *Courts*, for the great Improvement he made in that art." (Cf. *Parker's London News, or the Impartial Intelligencer*, March 27th, 1724.)

"On Friday last, the *Corpse* of *Daniel Quare*, the famous Watch-maker, was interr'd in the Quaker's Burying Ground in Bunhill Fields ; most of the Watch-makers in Town attended his Funeral." (Cf. *Ibid.*, March 30th.)

After Quare's death Horseman appears to have carried on the business in the original name of the partnership. In 1733 Horseman became bankrupt and the stock of the business realised.

"*To be Sold by* AUCTION.

"*Up Stairs at Garraway's Coffee-house, Exchange-Alley, for the Benefit of the Creditors of* Quare *and* Horseman.

"ALL the Clocks, Watches, Movements, Mathematical Instruments and Sun-Dials, &c. consisting of great Variety, that were taken by Statute of Bankrupt in the Dwelling-house of the celebrated Mr. Quare." (Cf. *The Daily Post.* April. 19, 1733.)

The small table clock illustrated in Fig. 119 is the work of William Webster I.

An advertisement of this maker in which he claims his connection with Thomas Tompion has already been quoted on page 136. The back plate of this clock bears the engraved inscription —*William Webster from ye late Mr Tho: Tompion London*—a further indication of Webster's wish to have his name connected with that of his late master.

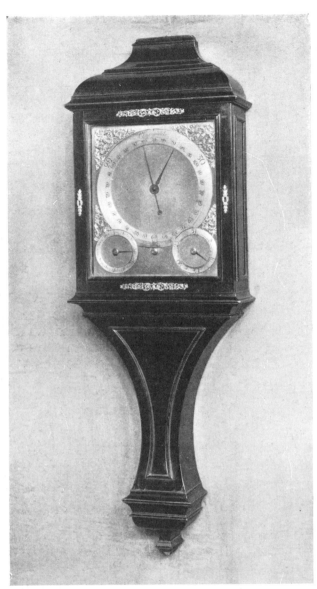

Fig. 120. A RARE MURAL WHEEL BAROMETER, by
GEORGE GRAHAM, ebonised pear-wood case with bracket.
Early 18th century

(Collection of J. S. Sykes, Esq.)

BAROMETERS

The mercurial barometer was an innovation of the time of Charles II. It was perfected during this reign by the researches of three distinguished scientists, Robert Boyle, Robert Hooke and Sir Samuel Moreland. These three men were assisted by clock and instrument makers, the most important of whom were Thomas Tompion, Daniel Quare and George Graham.

In the *Lives of the Norths* it is mentioned that Lord Keeper Guilford (1637-1685) took a considerable interest in the *Torricellian*

Experiment, and the measuring of the pressure of the atmosphere by means of a tube filled with mercury. He thought of the idea of marketing the barometer, an instrument at this period which was " confined to the cabinets of the virtuosi." In this project his lordship sought the assistance of Henry Jones, of the Temple, a watch- and clock-maker to whom he disclosed the method of the barometer's construction. Henry Jones is, therefore, said to have been the first to make and offer for sale the barometer in England.

In 1676 Robert Hooke mentions in his diary that that he " Cald on Thompion about new Barometer." At Hampton Court is a beautiful mural barometer by Tompion in a veneered mulberry case. It was made for William III and like the Royal clock illustrated Plate 8 it bears this King's cypher. The gilt metal brackets supporting the square dial of the barometer are of identical design to the brackets supporting the hood of the clock. Other features of similarity between the metal mounts of the barometer and those of the clock are the spandrel corners of the dial and the metal

Fig. 121. Mezzotint Portrait of GEORGE GRAHAM
(1673-1751)

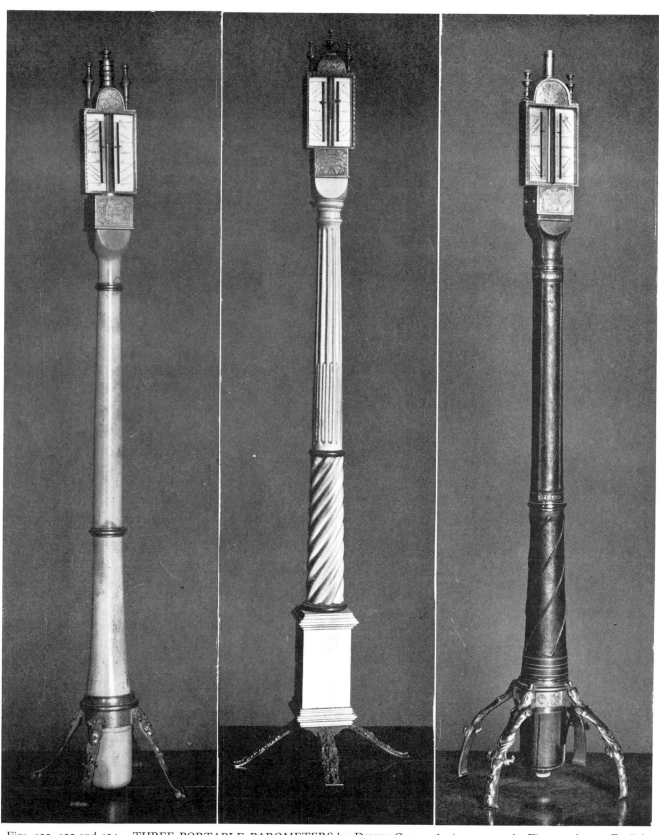

Figs. 122, 123 and 124. THREE PORTABLE BAROMETERS by DANIEL QUARE, the ivory example, Fig. 122, has an English and French scale. The example covered in leather, Fig. 124, is also fitted with a dual scale. *Circa* 1700

(*Collection of J. S. Sykes, Esq.*)

Fig. 125. DETAIL OF DIAL of portable ivory case
barometer, illustrated Fig. 122

moulding holding the glass of the dial door. Unquestionably both clock and barometer belong to the same period, and were supplied by Tompion for the furnishing of the new apartments at Hampton Court.

Daniel Quare is especially identified as a designer and maker of barometers. He invented a particular type of portable barometer, of which numerous examples are extant similar to the three illustrated, Figs. 122, 123 and 124.

"Daniel Quare, *Watchmaker, having invented a Portable Barometer or Weather Glass, which may be turned up side down without spoiling the Quick-silver, and yet the air operates as freely on it, as on the open ones now in use; which has been found very useful both by Sea and Land. His Majesty has been pleased to Grant to him Letters Pattens for the Sole making thereof. It having also been shewed before the Royal Society, who highly approved of it, and caused it to be entered into their Books as the first they had seen; which are Made and Sold by the said* Daniel Quare *at his Shop in* Exchange Alley *in* Cornhil." (Cf. *The London Gazette*, August 5th–8th, 1695.)

Quare's invention was a contrivance consisting of a pad to block the bottom of the mercury tube, thereby holding the quicksilver when the instrument was carried; the pad being brought into position by a screwed rod actuated at the base of the column, *vide* Fig. 127.

These portable barometers had two types of cases, one that stood on a table supported by hinged feet, similar to the examples illustrated, and one of the same design but without feet and made to hang on the wall.

Many more of the latter variety have survived than the former. Quare undoubtedly sold numbers of these portable weather glasses abroad; those made especially for export had a dual scale, one in French and the other in English, similar to the two examples illustrated. Unsigned examples of these barometers have also survived, but it would seem unlikely that few of these were made by Quare, being probably the work of imitators.

The treatments of the cases are varied; walnut examples are extant in far larger numbers than any other types. Examples of beech cases (ebonised or japanned) are to-day rare. Originally they were probably as popular, if not more so, as those of walnut, the perishable nature of japan work and beech-wood accounting for the fewer survivals. The barometer in the far more durable ivory case has survived in but few numbers, which signifies that originally ivory was reserved by Quare for the best and most expensive examples.

Fig. 126. DETAIL OF BASE OF IVORY BAROMETER with mercurial gilt supports, also illustrated in Fig. 122

163

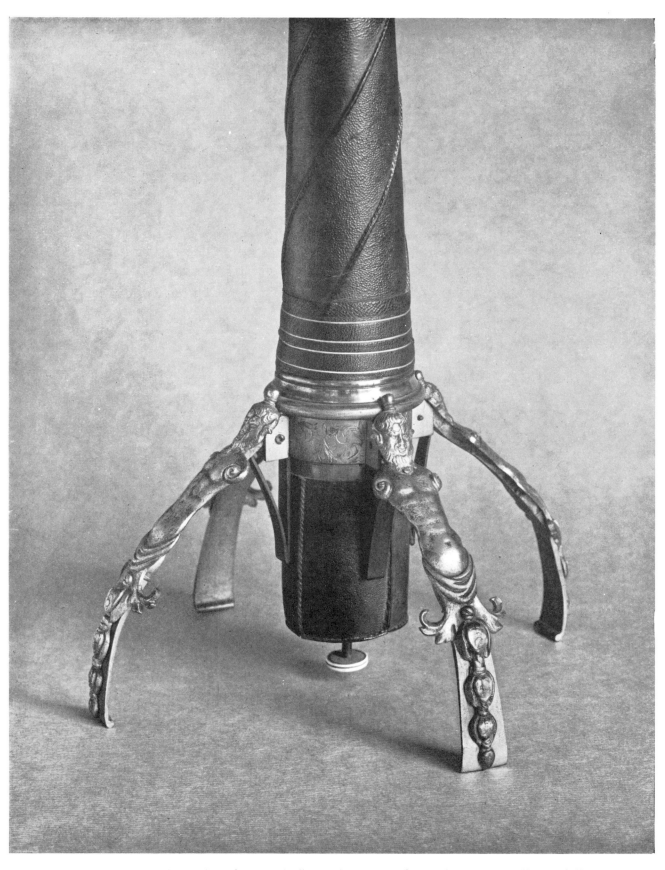

Fig. 127. DETAIL showing design of cast and gilt metal supports of portable barometer, illustrated Fig. 124

165

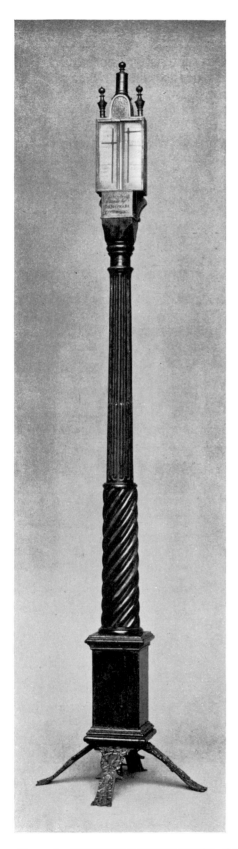

The two ivory-cased barometers, illustrated, are of exceptional quality, especially the one with the French and English scale. The mercurial gilding of the mounts makes a most pleasing contrast to the cream tint of the ivory. The example with a square base and spiral turning to the lower half of the column was of a favourite design, judging from the number that has survived.

The walnut cased barometer, Fig. 128 (which is of the same design as the ivory example, Fig. 123), has engraved on the side of the dial case the number 53. This suggests that Quare started to number these portable barometers, but as there are so many without numbers it would appear that for some reason he gave up the idea.

The barometer with the case covered with leather is unique as far as the writer is aware. The fine workmanship of the chased and gilt mercurial mounts (*vide* Fig. 127) and the engraving of the dial case indicate that this example was probably made to the special order of one of Quare's rich patrons. The mercurial gilt metal work was a feature that distinguished a barometer of the best quality from one of the more ordinary type which had the mounts of lacquered brass.

An interesting 18th century reference to one of Quare's portable barometers is contained in a catalogue of the sale of the Household Goods of Thomas Heath of Mile-End Green in the year 1742.

Fig. 128. PORTABLE BAROMETER, " invented and made by Dan. Quare London," in walnut case. The detail of foot shows unusual pattern. This barometer is numbered 53
(*Courtesy of J. M. Botibol, Esq.*)

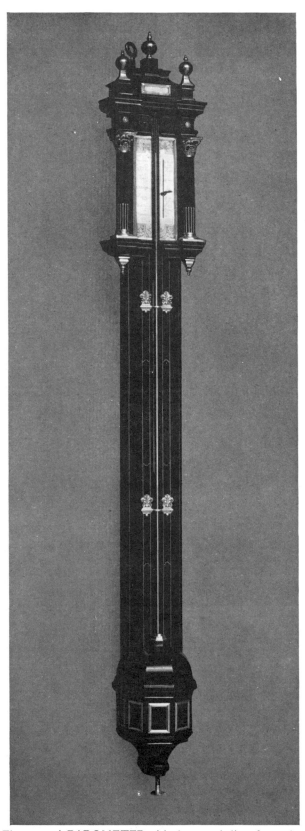

Fig. 129. A BAROMETER with ebony and silver frame, by Daniel Delander, which originally came from Clumber Castle. *Temp. :* Queen Anne.
(Collection of M. F. Moore, Esq.)

" A most curious weather glass by Quare, on brass feet, and a christal front."

The wheel barometer by George Graham, Fig. 120, is a rare instrument, as only few barometers have survived bearing this maker's name. The two small hand-operated circles at the base of the dial indicate the date of the day and the month. The design of the case with its attenuated bracket supporting the rectangular case is of especially pleasing proportions.

The maker of the barometer, Fig. 129, with its ebony and silver-mounted frame, was Daniel Delander. This maker, who it seems likely was of Huguenot descent, was in his early career a journeyman assistant of Thomas Tompion. He was admitted to the Clockmakers' Company in 1699, being apprenticed in 1692 to Charles Halsted. In 1706 he invented a safety catch for ladies' watch-cases ; this device he advertised in the *Post Man* of February 7th of that year :

" Whereas Ladies often lose their Watch-Cases from their sides, occasioned by the wearing of the Spring, This is to give Notice, that there is a new Invention of a Spring to fasten the Cases in such a manner that will infallible prevent being lost by Daniel Delander, Watch-maker in Devereaux-Court."

The following news item suggests that Delander had been guilty of a breach of the law :

" Mr. Delandre the Watchmaker is not to receive Sentence till the next Term "
(Cf. *The Evening Post*, February 7th, 1717.)

Delander had a lawsuit against the Duke of Chandos ; unfortunately it has not been possible to find any particulars concerning this action, which seems to have gone against the Duke.

" We hear the Duke of Chandois has brought his Writ of Error against the Judgement given in a Cause betwixt his Grace and Mr. Delander Watchmaker."
(Cf. *The Weekly Journal or Saturday's Post*, June 16th, 1722.)

Like Delander's clocks, the quality of the execution of the dial and mounts of the barometer illustrated is particularly good. The architectural design of the frame with its Corinthian columns and full entablature was especially favoured for barometers usually made of walnut in the first half of the 18th century. This barometer was originally at Clumber, from which house also came the looking-glass (one of a set of four) illustrated, Fig. 41.

Daniel Delander had a son, Nathaniel, who became Master of the Clockmakers' Company in 1747. There was also an earlier Nathaniel (admitted to the Clockmakers' Company in 1668), but it is uncertain what relationship he bore to Daniel.

The barometer in walnut case, Fig. 130, is an imposing example being 5 ft. in height. The name of the maker is Rice Williams; he specialised in "Air Pumps or Pneumatic Engines . . . Also Hydrostatical Fountains . . . Likewise curious wind Guns . . . Barometers, or Weather Glasses of all sorts, as Wheel, Diagonal, Portable or Marine . . . Recommended by the Royal Society . . . Curious Artificial Eyes . . . curiosities of all sorts in Pneumatics, Hydrostatics, Mechanics, Etc. and he lived " over against the Somerset House by the New Church in the Strand." In the above advertisement the mention of the various types of barometers is interesting. Rice Williams, although his name is not recorded as a clockmaker, appeared also to have made clocks as in a sale catalogue dated 1749—*A large and curious astronomical Clock, by* Rice Williams, *in a walnut-tree case*—is listed amongst the lots.

The diagonal barometer with mahogany frame, Fig. 131, is of a type which permits the smallest change in the atmosphere to be discernible; the mercury fluctuating to a far greater degree than in the barometer with a perpendicular tube. The centre panel which now contains a looking-glass plate, probably framed a printed perpetual calendar.

A number of diagonal barometers are extant dating from the first half of the 18th century; some have japan and others walnut frames, and the later specimens are framed in mahogany. According to an early 18th century advertisement of " J. Patrick in ye Old Baily London " this design of barometer is described:

LOOKING GLASS $\frac{\text{o}}{+}$ DIAGONAL BAROMETER.

" This moves 30 inches for Fair & Foul weather and hath on the right hand a Thermometer, Shewing 90 degrees between the greatest Heat & Cold and a large Looking-Glass in the middle."

It would seem that the earlier diagonal barometers with rectangular frames of this type had looking-glass plates and the later examples printed perpetual calendars. The diagonal barometer, which was sometimes termed a " Sign-Post " or a " Yard-Arm " barometer, was also mounted on a frame which followed the angle of the mercury tube.

Fig. 130. A BAROMETER AND THERMOMETER in walnut case, signed *Rice Williams Londoni fecit. Circa* 1740.
(*Collection of Geoffrey Blackwell, Esq., O.B.E.*)

Fig. 131. A DIAGONAL BAROMETER AND THERMOMETER mounted on mahogany
frame.   Maker unknown.   *Circa* 1750

(*Collection of Major Sir John Prestige*)

Label of a clock-case maker whose craft was an individual trade in the late 17th and 18th centuries. (*Courtesy of Malcolm Webster, Esq.*)

INDEX